THE COLLECTED WRITINGS OF JACK COTTRELL

VOLUME I

THE UNITY
OF TRUTH

JACK COTTRELL

THE CHRISTIAN RESTORATION ASSOCIATION

TABLE OF CONTENTS

PREFACE

My first published writing was my brief valedictory speech, given at the Cincinnati Bible Seminary graduation in 1959. Brother R. E. Elmore, then the director of the Christian Restoration Association (the CRA), and editor of *The Restoration Herald*, came up to me after the ceremony. He praised me for the speech, entitled "The Call To Build." He asked if I would let him publish it in the *Herald*. Well, obviously, since it was so good, and since he wanted it so badly, I could not say no. So it appeared in the October 1959 issue of *The Restoration Herald*.

Later I was talking with one of my favorite CBS professors, Brother Tom Friskney; and I told him that Brother Elmore had actually requested me to allow him to print my masterpiece in the *Herald*. Brother Friskney gently took that opportunity to teach me a lesson in humility. He said, "Oh, he always asks all the graduation speakers to let him print their speeches."

Well, even though my ego-bubble was appropriately popped, it was still quite satisfying to see my material in print!

It has been nearly sixty years since then, and in that period of time I would guess that close to 200 of my writings have been published in one form or another. (I do not have an official list.) This includes (as of May 2018) twenty-three books of various sizes, a few chapters written for other books, and scores of articles in periodicals. This is not counting file drawers here in my home office that are filled with outlines of speeches, lessons, sermons, and courses taught over my 48 years of teaching at CBS. (I composed and taught over 40 courses altogether.)

I have been thinking recently that some of this (non-book) material might be found useful if were published in book form; so I have decided to spend some time on this as a project. I do not know how far I will get, since I am just now turning 80 years old. Anyway, this present book is the first volume in a projected series that I am calling "The Collected Works of Jack Cottrell." I will focus mainly on articles that have already been printed in periodicals, plus outlines of speeches as yet unpublished.

I am grateful to the CRA for its growing interest in publishing, and for doing the detailed work of publishing these volumes.

I am calling this first volume *The Unity of Truth*. A main theme of my whole career has been TRUTH; thus it seems appropriate to begin with this subject. The lead essay has the same title as the book, namely, "The Unity of Truth." This is a brand new study, never before published. In length, it is sort of in between an essay and a book, so I will call it a "theologella" for three reasons. First, it is about theology. Second, short novels are called novellas; the length of this piece fits that pattern. Third, I like to make up new words.

The next three studies herein are of different lengths. Two have been published before, both in *The Restoration Herald*. One is called "In Matters of Faith, Unity; in Matters of Opinion, Liberty." This goes back to the February/March 2009 issues of the *Herald*. The other is a slightly longer version of a piece called "Christian Truth for a World in Decay," which appeared twice in the *Herald*: in the December 2016 issue, and in the June/July 2017 issues. The next piece here is entitled "'Hold On!' The Tyranny of Change." This is a sermon first preached at the Greendale (IN) First Church of Christ (where I worship and work), then for a chapel service at the (then) Florida Christian College. This is its first time in print.

The next item is "The Peter Pan Syndrome: Churches and Christians That Won't Grow Up." This is one of my favorite compositions. I have presented it numerous times, beginning at a meeting in Louisville, KY, in 2014. It is based solely on Paul's teaching in Ephesians 4:11-16. Next is my most recent composition (as of May 14, 2018). I was asked to speak on this subject for the April 2018 meeting of the Fi-County Ministerial Association in Mowrystown, OH, namely, "Is the Restoration Movement Still Relevant?" My answer is yes, but only if we decide to put faithfulness to God's truth ahead of our quest for the unity of Christendom. This applies especially to the truth about baptism.

The final entry here is a paper I presented in Indianapolis, IN, in the fall of 1989, at a conference on the nature of Biblical authority sponsored by the Christian Theological Seminary (Disciples of Christ). Three main speakers were invited to present papers on the conservative, moderate, and liberal perspectives on this subject. I was asked to present a paper from the conservative viewpoint. All of the proceedings from this conference were originally published as *Conservative, Moderate, Liberal: The Biblical Authority Debate,* ed. Charles R. Blaisdell (St. Louis: CBP Press, 1990). My paper is on pp. 21-40 therein, and is reprinted here by permission, with thanks to the editor.

I will here note that almost all of my Scripture quotations are either from the New American Standard Bible (1995), or the English Standard Version.

I am in the process of planning the next volume, which will probably be called *God's Word Is Truth.* It will be a selection of pieces on Biblical themes. Meanwhile, I hope you enjoy this one.

JACK COTTRELL
May 14, 2018

SECTION ONE

THE UNITY
OF TRUTH

THE UNITY OF TRUTH

INTRODUCTION

Many think the Restoration Movement is defined by how it relates the two concepts of UNITY and TRUTH. Once we accept this as a valid observation, we are immediately encountered with this problem: there does not seem to be any agreement on HOW these two concepts are related. Are they in *opposition*? I.e., do we have to choose between them: unity OR truth? Or are they in *tension*? Are both valid, but uncomfortable together? Or are they *independent*? Are both valid, but unrelated to one another: unity AND truth? Or are they a *natural combination,* somehow inherently inseparable and interdependent? If we choose this last option, we still must answer, HOW are they combined?

To some degree, how we answer such questions depends on how we define the terms. First, what do we mean by "unity"? One possibility is organizational union, in which all congregations are bound together by membership in the same governing body and by submission to a common set of by-laws. This is not the point of Biblical church unity, though. The Restoration Movement has always been committed to congregational church polity. Each congregation is governed by its own group of elders. This does not prevent cooperation among congregations, however, which opens the door to the following.

Another possible definition is unity in the sense of missional cooperation, where all who wear the name Christian work together in acts and programs of service to the community and defense of the common Christian world view. This applies to both congregations and individuals. For example, we in the Restoration Movement can cooperate with Catholics and other Protestants, with Baptists and Methodists, and with other Christian groups in promoting such things as the pro-life movement, creationist efforts, and alliances that defend the Biblical view of marriage and family. This is a valid approach to unity, but it is not what we usually mean when we use the term.

A third possibility is that Christian unity is the common spiritual oneness shared by all individuals who have properly obeyed the gospel by believing, repenting, confessing Christ as Lord and Savior, and being baptized into a saving union with Christ. This is genuine "one body" Christian unity (Ephesians 4:4); however, it is not something we have to seek, because it is already a reality established by God and not by man (Acts 2:47). Our duty is simply to acknowledge it and accept it.

A final kind of unity is *doctrinal agreement*, in which all Christians agree on what is the one right meaning of Biblical teaching. Most Christians accept the idea that this kind of unity must exist with reference to at least a few crucial doctrines, usually described as "salvation issues." But what about all other Biblical teaching? The tendency in our time is to refer all "non-salvation issues" to the category of opinions, and to exclude them from the category of beliefs for which agreement is possible or necessary (i.e., "the essentials"). In this essay I will be focusing on this *kind* of unity, i.e., unity of doctrinal agreement, but I will be opposing this popular version of it. Instead, I will be defending this thesis: The Bible itself requires all Christians to have a UNITY OF TRUTH, i.e., to agree on what is the one right meaning of *all* Biblical teaching. Such a unity is obviously not a reality, but it should be our deliberate goal.

The other term that must be defined is "truth." Here I will not be examining various philosophical definitions of the word. I will proceed with the assumption that the only valid concept of truth is what is called the correspondence theory. I.e., a statement is true if it corresponds to reality. No other way of defining truth does justice to the word. So what other approach to truth are we pursuing here? Having accepted the correspondence definition of truth, our purpose here is to determine what, within the context of Christian doctrine, should be the SCOPE of the "truth" (doctrinal agreement) upon which we should be united.

Here are several possibilities, moving from the most limited to the most comprehensive. First, some would say that the only Biblical teachings we must agree on are those having to do with JESUS, i.e., teachings by Jesus and/or about Jesus. I reject this as a much too narrow scope for doctrinal agreement; it is not consistent with either the Bible's view of Jesus and his work, or the Bible's teaching about itself. It is an example of what I call the Christological fallacy, i.e., trying to make Jesus into an epistemological norm rather than the one who redeems us from sin.

A second approach to the scope of truth would be to limit it to those issues we could call the GOSPEL, which is another way of describing the "salvation issues" mentioned above. This view says that we must agree especially on the Bible's teaching on how to be saved. I certainly agree with this, but I believe that it is too limited. Many things that are not essential to believe for salvation are essential for other aspects of Christian faith and practice, and for life in general. Thus the scope of truth must be broader than this.

A third approach is to say that we must count as truth everything that is part of the Christian WORLD VIEW as a whole, e.g., everything having to do with God and creation, the nature and purpose of human beings, the reality of sin and salvation, ethics and holy living, and life after death. This list is quite inclusive, and we definitely should be united in what we believe about such things. But this is still not comprehensive enough.

The final and correct approach to the scope of the truth about which we should have unity is this: the contents of the Bible as a whole and in general. This is indeed the correct view, and I will defend it here. The main reason why I believe this is because of the very nature of the Bible. If the Bible is what it says it is, and what we believe it is, namely, the very WORD OF GOD, then we cannot come to any other conclusion. Thus in a real sense, the most fundamental question we can ask is this: "What is the nature of the Bible?" This is our starting point. How we answer this question will affect everything else we believe and do.

The Restoration Movement from its beginning has emphasized the importance of the Bible. Most of our defining principles are about the Bible, as is seen in our familiar slogans. E.g., "the Bible alone is our only rule of faith and practice" (our version of *sola Scriptura*). "Where the Bible speaks, we speak; where the Bible is silent, we are silent." "No book but the Bible; no creed but Christ; no name but the divine." "Call Bible things by Bible names; do Bible things in Bible ways."

If I were writing a book (or a *set* of books!) on this subject, it would go like this: PART ONE: What is the Bible? What does it claim to be? Answer: the inspired, inerrant Word of God. This is the *bibliology* segment of systematic theology. It answers the "what's so" question. PART TWO: How do we know this is true? Answer: by examining the available evidence. This is what we call *apologetics*. It answers the "how do we know" question. PART THREE: what is the significance of possessing a book that is the Word of God? If the Bible is indeed the Word of God, then *what else* must be true? This answers the "so what" question.

In this essay I plan to summarize the contents of parts one and three in the previous paragraph. For our present purposes I will assume that we can successfully establish part two. (For a brief treatment of the material in part one and the assumed material in part two, see my small book *Solid: The Authority of God's Word*, previously published by Standard Publishing, Baker Book House, and College Press; now published by Wipf and Stock Publishers. See also chapter 2, "Our Knowledge of God," pp. 44-66 in my book *The Faith Once for All*, published by College Press.)

Here my main purpose is to affirm NINE fundamental truths about the Bible and our relationship to it. These nine truths progressively build upon one another logically, one after the other. These will be established here by showing the Bible's own teaching about them. I will be heading toward this conclusion: we must not speak of "unity OR truth." We must not speak *only* of "unity AND truth," or "unity WITH truth," or "unity IN truth." We must pursue the UNITY **OF** TRUTH.

PART ONE
NINE THESES

Before going to the main body of this essay, I will here first simply list the nine theses, the nine fundamental truths, that establish the validity of the concept of the unity of truth. Each one is accompanied by a few of the Biblical texts that support it.

ONE. The Bible is the Word of God. 2 Samuel 23:2; Romans 3:2; 1 Thessalonians 2:13; 2 Timothy 3:16.

TWO. Because the Bible is the Word of God, it is TRUE in every statement, assertion, or affirmation that it makes. Proverbs 30:5; John 10:35; John 17:17; Titus 1:2; 1 John 3:20.

THREE. The Bible is God's personal communication to His human creatures. 1 Corinthians 10:11; 2 Timothy 3:16-17.

FOUR. When God communicates with us in the Bible in human language, He intends for everything He says to have one specific true and right meaning. Isaiah 55:11; 1 Corinthians 14:9-10.

FIVE. God intends and expects us human beings to know and UNDERSTAND the one specific true and right meaning of Scripture. Matthew 22:37 (Mark 12:33); 2 Corinthians 1:13-14; Colossians 1:9-10; Hebrews 4:12.

SIX. We CAN understand this one true and right meaning of Scripture, because we have been created in the image of God. Ephesians 4:23-24; Colossians 3:9-10.

SEVEN. We as human beings not only CAN understand the one true and right meaning of Scripture; we are under MORAL OBLIGATION to do so, i.e., NOT to understand the one true meaning of Scripture is a sin. Matthew 13:1-23; Matthew 15:10; Ephesians 5:17; 2 Timothy 2:15; 2 Timothy 2:25-26.

EIGHT. We must not only understand and believe the one true and right meaning of Scripture; we must actually HOLD FAST to this understanding with full assurance, confidence, and conviction. 1 Corinthians 11:2; Colossians 2:2; Colossians 4:12; 2 Thessalonians 2:15; 2 Timothy 3:14; Titus 1:9; Titus 3:8; Hebrews 10:22-23.

NINE. If all the above are true, then we must conclude that it is God's preceptive will that all Christians have a UNITY of belief and truth — that we all hold to the SAME UNDERSTANDING of the one true and right meaning of all Biblical teaching. 1 Corinthians 1:10; 2 Corinthians 13:11; Ephesians 4:12-13; Philippians 1:27; Philippians 2:2; 1 Peter 3:8.

PART TWO
EXPLANATION OF THE THESES

THESIS ONE

The Bible is the Word of God.

The Bible originally was (and still is) written in the words of human languages — Hebrew, Aramaic, and Greek. In human experience in general, languages (words, sentences) are used to communicate ideas and concepts from the mind of one person to the mind of another person (or other persons). What is the ultimate origin of the words of the Bible? Whose ideas and concepts are they meant to communicate, and to whom? Is God involved in this process in some way?

Those who deny that God exists or deny that he is personally involved in earthly affairs necessarily exclude God from any explanation of the Bible's origin and existence. To them the Bible, and even the very phenomena of human language as such, are the result of unguided chance evolution and human speculation.

This is not how the Bible explains itself, however. In every way, the Bible claims to be the Word of God — indeed, "the very words of God" (Romans 3:2, NIV). Language itself is pictured as existing in the mind of God, even before any human beings were created. See the "Let there be" pronouncements in Genesis 1:1-25. See the intra-Trinitarian declaration in Genesis 1:26, "Let Us make man in Our image." This image of God must have included an inherent ability to use language, and an inherent knowledge of the specific language already present in God's mind. We know this because God began speaking to Adam and Eve as soon as they were created. See Genesis 2:16-17, and Genesis 1:28-30. (Unless otherwise specified, quotations from the Bible are herein taken from the New American Standard Bible, or NASB.)

God speaking to human beings in human language is one form of what is called *revelation*. God actually reveals Himself (unveils Himself, makes Himself known) in several different ways (see my *Faith Once for All*, pp. 44-49), but word revelation is the most precise and the most efficient form of revelation. In the Bible, from beginning to end, God is pictured as speaking to human beings: to Adam and Eve, to Cain, to Noah and his sons, to Abraham, to Isaac, to Jacob, to Moses and to the host of prophets who followed him, and on many occasions recorded in the New Testament.

In revealing Himself, sometimes God spoke to people directly, both to individuals (see Exodus 3:4ff.) and to groups (see Exodus 20 and Matthew 3:17). When Jesus as God in the flesh spoke to those around Him, this was always a form of direct revelation, both from God the Father and from God the Son. John 3:34 says, "He whom God has sent speaks the words of God." This makes it clear that the words of Jesus ARE the words of God.

But usually God spoke indirectly, first delivering His message to an individual (angelic or human), who then was appointed to pass it along to others. Those who thus spoke for God were called *prophets*, a word that literally means "one who speaks on behalf of another." Because they were literally speaking God's message ("Thus says the LORD . . ."), the words of the prophets were still *God's* words; their message was *the Word of God*.

The same is true of the apostles. Jesus said in His prayer to the Father that He passed the Father's words along to his Apostles: "For the words which You gave Me I have given to them; and they received them and truly understood .... I have given them Your word" (John 17:8, 14). After

Jesus's resurrection and His ascension to His heavenly throne, He continued to speak through His apostles as they were aided by the Holy Spirit (John 16:13-15). Thus the teachings of the apostles were the words of God the Father and of God the Son.

The writer of the Letter to the Hebrews sums up the reality of revelation: "God ... spoke long ago to the fathers in the prophets," and now he "has spoken to us in His Son. ... See to it that you do not refuse Him who is speaking" (Hebrews 1:1-2; 12:25).

How does this relate to the Bible? The point is that God's revelation in the form of words can be delivered not just orally, but also in writing! And the Bible, as written words, represents itself over and over as being God's revealed Word in written form. See for example Romans 3:2, where Paul refers to the Old Testament as *to logia tou theou*, "The very words of God" (NIV). Thus the fact of word revelation is a major reason for calling the Bible the Word of God.

This analysis of the Bible as a form of revelation leaves us with two serious questions, however. For one thing, the Biblical words of revelation are, by the very nature of Scripture, being passed along to us (in the original texts) by human writers. How can we be sure that these human writers have done this accurately, without corrupting the message? For another thing, strictly speaking, only some parts of the Bible are actually revelation — messages from God being passed along by prophets. What about non-revealed sections, such as historical records, genealogies, and personal testimonies? Not everything in the Bible, in its original context, is represented as part of a message being passed on through a prophet. In what sense can such material be called the Word of God? And why should we trust it?

These questions are answered by the Bible's testimony to another form of divine activity that affects the nature of the Bible, namely, *inspiration*. God's Word comes to us not only through divine revelation, but also through divine inspiration. (See my *Faith Once for All*, pp. 50-57.) In the Bible God is entrusting the Biblical writers to pass His revelation along accurately to all readers. He is also enabling them to be absolutely accurate in recording for us all the other kinds of data contained in the Bible. What is God doing that guarantees the accuracy of all the contents of the Bible? Specifically, when the Biblical writers are in the process of writing the words of the Bible, God is exerting a power or an influence on them in a way that guarantees that what they say will be what God wants it to be. This influence is what we call inspiration.

The result of this influence is this: some parts of the Bible are revealed and some are not, but ALL parts of the Bible are divinely inspired. Because of inspiration, every word of the original writings of the Bible is of divine origin and thus has God's "stamp of approval." When we speak of the "divine origin" of Scripture, we are including both of these divine actions: revelation and inspiration.

The Biblical teaching about inspiration is abundant. David, the shepherd-king who wrote many of the Psalms, says this about his writing: "The Spirit of the LORD spoke by me, and His word was on my tongue" (2 Samuel 23:2). Jesus acknowledges this when He declares that David spoke the words of Psalm 110:1 "in the Spirit," i.e., when he was under the influence of the Holy Spirit.

After referring to the "sacred writings" of the Old Testament in 2 Timothy 3:15, Paul then in verse 16 speaks of "all Scripture" — not just the Old Testament but the New Testament as well — as being "God-breathed," or breathed out by God. Sometimes this is translated "inspired by God," but the Greek word is *theopneustos* and literally means "God-breathed." This means that when the human authors were engaged in the process of writing the Biblical texts, whether revealed or otherwise, the Holy Spirit was so supervising and guarding their minds and their hands that the result was as if their message had come from the very heart and hand of God. The Spirit was in such control that whatever they wrote was as accurate and trustworthy as if it had been breathed out of the very mouth of God. (See Matthew 4:4.)

The Apostle Peter specifically attributes this divine influence to God the Holy Spirit. He says in 2 Peter 1:20-21, "Above all, you must understand that no prophecy of Scripture came about by the prophet's own interpretation of things. For prophecy never had its origin in the human will, but prophets, though human, spoke from God as they were carried along by the Holy Spirit." (This is the NIV translation, which should be used in order to avoid some common wrong interpretations of these verses.) What is Peter saying here? He affirms that what the Biblical writers said was not their own interpretation of things; they did not decide on their own to sit down and write a part of the Bible. Rather, the Holy Spirit was in control of the writing process.

The New Testament says much more about its own inspiration, but we will call attention here only to Jesus's promises to His apostles in John's gospel. Concerning their general teaching Jesus promised that the Spirit "will teach you all things, and bring to your remembrance all that I said to you" (John 14:26). Here the first promise refers to new revelation; the second means that they would have infallible memories of what Jesus had already taught them (which is an aspect of inspiration). In John 16:13 Jesus specifically promises the apostles (not Christians in general) that "when He, the Spirit of truth, comes, He will guide you into all the truth." Jesus declares that this truth would ultimately be coming from Himself through the Spirit (see vv. 12-15). The apostolic writings of the New Testament are part of the fulfillment of these promises.

One of the amazing things about inspiration is that God could exert this influence upon the Biblical writers without making their own minds go blank and suppressing their own thought processes. When He was revealing material such as predictive prophecies (e.g., Psalm 45, Isaiah 53) and doctrinal truth known only to Him (e.g., Genesis 1:1ff.; John 1:1ff.), we can understand that He was probably dictating the very words the writers used (see 1 Corinthians 2:9-13). But much of the Bible's content was produced at least in part from the human writers' own experiences, feelings, and contemplations (e.g., Habakkuk 1:12-2:1; Acts 21:1-6). In such cases the Spirit's inspiration enabled these writers to speak their own words without including errors and without omitting whatever God wanted to be included.

When we consider all of the Bible's testimony to its own divine origin, we conclude that it is no wonder that we consider it to be the Word of God. We remember David's testimony that "the Spirit of the LORD spoke by me, and His word was on my tongue" (2 Samuel 23:2). Jeremiah knew his writings to be the words of God (Jeremiah 36:2), just as Paul calls the Old Testament "the very words of God" (Romans 3:2). Paul knew that his teachings were the Word of God. He reminds the Thessalonians (1 Thessalonians 2:13) that "when you received the word of God which you heard from us, you accepted it not as the word of men, but for what it really is, the word of God."

THESIS TWO

The Bible is True in Every Respect.

The fact that the Bible was written under the influence of divine inspiration results in its nature or character as the Word of God. And just because it is GOD'S Word, it is TRUE. As Jesus says in His long prayer to God recorded in John 17, "Sanctify them in the truth; Your word is truth" (v. 17). God's Word is TRUTH!

(Technically this applies to the sentences in the Bible that are actually making a statement of fact, i.e., a statement or proposition that claims to be describing an aspect of reality — often called a truth-claim. I am simply pointing out that other kinds of sentences have other purposes, i.e., to issue a command, to ask a question, or to express an emotion. Sentences such as these do not intend to make a claim to be *true*. When we affirm that the Bible is true, we are mainly referring only to its truth-claims. This point is not a matter of dispute.)

We can assert that the Bible is true; we can also say this in other ways and mean the same thing. We can say that it is trustworthy, that it is reliable, that it is correct, that it is pure, that it is *inerrant*. This last word ("inerrant") has often been unjustly attacked and rejected, but saying the Bible is inerrant is no different from saying that it is true. If all of its statements of fact are true, then it is without error, i.e., it is inerrant. (For a fuller discussion of this, see my book, *The Faith Once for All*, pp. 57-64.)

Another word that is appropriately used of Scripture is that it is *infallible*. This is not exactly the same as inerrant. To say that the Bible is infallible means that it *cannot* make a mistake, simply because it is the

Word of God. And because it is infallible (incapable of error), it is in fact inerrant (without error).

Besides John 17:17, where in the Bible do we see its own claims to be absolutely true, i.e., inerrant? We can cite Proverbs 30:5, which declares that "Every word of God is flawless" (NIV; see Psalm 18:30). The Hebrew word translated "flawless" means "to test, to refine, to purify," as in the purifying or testing of precious metals. In other words, when challenged or put to the test, "every word of God proves true" (as the NRSV translates Proverbs 30:5). In Romans 3:4 Paul says something similar: "Let God be found true, though every man be found a liar, as it is written, 'That You may be justified in Your words, and prevail when You are judged' [citing Psalm 51:4]."

Another affirmation of the Bible's truth or inerrancy is the statement of Jesus in John 10:35, "The Scripture cannot be broken." He says this after citing Psalm 82:6 in an argument with His Jewish enemies. In other words He is saying, "My argument is sound because it is based on Scripture, and Scripture cannot be destroyed, refuted, found faulty, found untrue, disproved, challenged, or denied." We should note that Jesus's statement is about the nature of the written Word (i.e., Scripture) as a whole, or the Bible in general. The point Jesus makes is this: *just because it is in Scripture*, we know it cannot be broken; it *has* to be true.

That God's words *must* be true, in the sense that they are without error, is a necessary inference of the Bible's testimony about the very nature of God. Titus 1:2 says that God "cannot lie"; thus there can be no *deliberate* errors in the Bible. Also, 1 John 3:20 says that God "knows all things"; i.e., He is omniscient. Thus there can be no *accidental* errors in His words. Therefore every word He speaks must be true. This is why we describe the Bible as *infallible.*

We should remember that this character of inerrancy or absolute truthfulness applies only to the original text of Scripture as it was written or approved in its original languages by its original authors, the prophets of God and the apostles of Jesus Christ. Thanks to the science of textual criticism, we know with few exceptions what this original text was, even though we do not have the original manuscripts themselves. This truthfulness applies to translations of this original text into other languages, insofar as they accurately represent the original text.

All that I have said here has already been summarized in a statement of faith adopted during one era in the history of the graduate school at Cincinnati Christian University. This statement of faith said this: "All Scripture, as first written by the authors themselves, was produced under the direct inspiration of the Holy Spirit. Scripture is therefore the Word of God in written form, and is infallible and inerrant in its entirety when taken in the original meaning of its authors. Thus it is the sole and sufficient rule for faith and practice."

Why is it important to understand that the Bible is inerrant? A principal reason is that it is crucial to the very purpose for reading the Bible in the first place. We read the Bible because we want to understand God's revelation to us, along with all the other truths His Word contains, so that we can have a correct understanding of all things contained in the Christian world view. We believe that this correct understanding is found in the Bible. But if we deny the inerrancy of the Bible, we give up our one objective reference point for truth and sound doctrine as such. On the other hand, when we accept the Bible as inerrant, it stands before us as an objective standard of truth. The only requirements for sound doctrine are good textual criticism, correct translation, and proper exegesis. Meeting these challenges is daunting enough, but if the Bible is not inerrant, then a more basic requirement intrudes: one must also decide which Biblical statements are true and thus authoritative for true doctrine, and which are tainted with error and thus useless for truth.

The problem is clear. If one denies Biblical inerrancy, he is saying there are errors in the Bible — *somewhere*. But how does he know where? There is no comprehensive way to answer this question. Whatever criterion one uses for making such a decision will be subjective; he will wind up believing what he wants to believe and rejecting what he does not want to believe. The results of such subjectivism will be a mystical faith, doctrinal relativism, and in the end doctrinal agnosticism.

When we communicate verbally with one another, the importance of the accuracy of that communication depends on the importance of the subject matter about which we are communicating. Vacation postcards could contain errors of fact, and little would depend on it. If a road map (or GPS instruction) is wrong, it may be inconvenient but not fatal. On the other hand, mistakes in medical prescriptions or in military communications could be matters of life or death. But the Biblical message is in a category by itself; it is obviously the most important communication of all, since it is a matter of *eternal* life and *eternal* death. It is a message of such importance that God has not entrusted it to fallible memories and understandings. He has personally made sure that it reaches us without error.

In this section we have attempted to show that the Bible teaches its own absolute truthfulness; it claims to be infallible and without error. But why should we believe these claims? We cannot simply reply, "Because the Bible says so." That would be arguing in a circle. The answer basically is, "Because the relevant evidence shows that the claims are true." Examining the relevant evidence is the task of what is called *apologetics*, or Christian evidences. This material cannot be covered in this brief study. A condensed presentation of the reasons why we should believe the Bible are given in my small book, *Solid: The Authority of God's Word*, now published by Wipf and Stock. See especially chapters 6-8.

THESIS THREE

The Bible is God's personal communication to His human creatures.

We have seen that God communicates to human beings by means of revelation. Even when this revelation is mediated to us through prophets and apostles, it is the *Word of God*. In this section we will see that this applies even when (or especially when) God's communicated message comes to us in *written* form. In the New Testament the Greek word translated "Scripture" is *graphē*, which literally means "something written, the writing." (The verb is *graphō*, "to write.") Thus the very word we use for the Bible — "Scripture" — emphasizes its written nature.

Some writings are not necessarily directed toward any specific audience, or any audience at all. Someone might write just to put her thoughts down on paper, e.g., in a diary. Someone might write just to express his feelings, e.g., in poetry. On one level this may be true of some parts of the Bible, e.g., some Psalms. But in the final analysis, the Bible in all its parts is ultimately written to and for the entire audience of human beings in general.

In what sense is this true — that the Bible is God's intentional communication with human beings? It is not addressed to the entire human race in the form of a letter — "To whom it may concern ...." In the immediate sense, most parts of the Bible are directed to specific individuals or groups for specific purposes. E.g., some parts are addressed to God Himself, such as Psalms of praise (e.g., Psalm 99) and prophetic prayers (e.g., Psalm 51; Habakkuk 3). Some other parts are addressed to specific individuals, such as Timothy, Titus, Philemon, and Theophilus (cf. Luke 1:1-4; Acts 1:1). Some are written for specific groups of people, i.e., the Law of Moses was written specifically for the Jews, and most of Paul's letters were directed to specific churches.

But ultimately, every part of the Bible is written and intended for all human beings, in the sense that it is intended to be used by all who will do so. This means that the Bible is actually written on two levels: most of the time to a specific audience, but ALL of the time to the whole world. This is true because every part of the Bible by its very nature has two authors. One is the human author, who usually has a specific and more limited audience in mind; the other is the divine author, God Himself, who is intending for the Bible to be received by and used by all of us in the human race. This dual authorship is the result of the divine works of revelation and inspiration, as explained above.

My point here is that it is no accident that we have a BOOK that we rightly call the Word of God; that book is the BIBLE (from Greek *biblos*, sometimes *biblion*, both meaning — "book"!). This book is not just some human invention or compilation of scattered human writings. As Peter says, "No prophecy was ever made by an act of human will, but men moved by the Holy Spirit spoke from God" (2 Peter 1:21). Note: "FROM GOD!" The Bible is God's idea. His purpose for it is to communicate His truth to us human beings, whom He made for the very purpose of fellowship, communion and communication between Himself and us.

Sometimes in the distant past, God spoke to some human beings directly, using human speech in oral communication. But His *main* communication with us is in written form. The Bible communicates to us what God wants us to know, even what He wants to say to us from the depths of His own heart (1 Corinthians 2:9-13). Every time we open our Bibles and read something from it, it is like getting a letter or email from God! And we can think of our Bibles as being sent to us as a gift from God, wrapped in a package that is addressed to "The Human Race," or addressed specifically to the individual reading it (e.g., Jackie Cottrell, R.R. #3, Stamping Ground, Kentucky)!

That the Bible is intended to be God's communication to His people in all ages is seen in many specific texts. For example, Paul shows us in 1 Corinthians 10 that the records of Israel's history under the Old Covenant were written for our sakes and directed to us. The things that happened to the Israelites in their wilderness wanderings "happened as examples for us," says Paul (v. 6). Even their sins and punishments "happened to them as an example, and they were written for our instruction" (v. 11). Paul also cites Deuteronomy 25:4 and applies it to Christian living, saying "For our sake it was written" (1 Corinthians 9:10). So the Pentateuch was not just for the Jews, but was also God's communication even to us Christians, giving us some lessons on how to live! (This is not to say, however, that the Law of Moses as such is meant to be followed by anyone after the Old Covenant came to an end.)

Paul tells us something similar about the Genesis account of Abraham as the prime example of one who was justified by faith. God made sure this was recorded in Scripture for our benefit! Paul says, "Now not for his sake only was it written that it was credited to him, but for our sake also, to whom it will be credited, as those who believe in Him who raised Jesus our Lord from the dead" (Romans 4:23-24). It was written *for our sake*!

The Apostle Peter, in 1 Peter 1:10-12, says the same thing about all the Old Testament prophecies of the coming and the work of Jesus Christ. The Old Testament prophets themselves, he says, did not understand the point of great prophecies, such as Psalm 110, Isaiah 53, and Daniel 7:13-14. They searched and searched to find out what these Spirit-inspired prophecies were all about, but, "It was revealed to them that they were not serving themselves, but you, in these things which now have been announced to you through those who preached the gospel to you by the Holy Spirit sent from heaven" (v. 12). These prophecies were God's message to us! (See 2 Peter 1:19.)

The Apostle Paul sums this up in Romans 15:4 when he says, "For whatever was written in earlier times was written for our instruction, so that through perseverance and the encouragement of the Scriptures we might have hope."

No wonder we have such a thing as the Bible! No wonder God made sure that most of the Old Testament prophets wrote their messages down in permanent form (see Jeremiah 36). No wonder God told the Apostle John a dozen times in the Book of Revelation to WRITE the things being revealed to him, e.g., "And He said, 'Write, for these words are faithful and true'" (21:5). No wonder the New Testament around 80 times cites the Old Testament and declares, "It is written!"

Considering the Bible as a whole, we can ask, WHY did God want to speak these words to us? What is His purpose? What is He intending to accomplish thereby? These questions are answered in 2 Timothy 3:16-17, which says, "All Scripture is inspired by God [lit., "God-breathed"] and profitable for teaching, for reproof, for correction, for training in righteousness; so that the man of God may be adequate, equipped for every good work." Verse 16 specifically says that ALL Scripture, i.e., both Old and New Testaments, is *breathed out* by God, which is literally what happens when one speaks words in human language. This is a way of saying that every Scripture (every "sacred writing," v. 15) is the Word of God.

Verses 16-17 proceed to tell us why God has given us this unspeakable gift. Here Paul says that Scripture is "profitable" for certain things. The word "profitable" is *ōphelimos* (the next to last word in my Arndt & Gingrich Greek lexicon!), meaning "beneficial, useful, helpful, advantageous." This word introduces God's *purpose* (or *purposes*, plural) for giving us the Bible. So, exactly what is it profitable or useful FOR? Paul lists four things.

First, Scripture is given to us by God for teaching or doctrine (Greek, *didaskalia*). This is its most general purpose; and it includes teaching about all aspects of God's truth, or the full spectrum of systematic theology. It also includes teaching about ethics or holy living. It is the "sound *doctrine*" (same word) mentioned in 1 Timothy 1:10; Titus 1:9; 2:1, among other places.

Second, Scripture is given to bring about *elegmos* in our lives. This word is used only here in the New Testament. It is basically the opposite of the first purpose, which is to give us instruction in *truth*. *Elegmos*, though, refers to giving us instruction in *error* and wrongdoing. Here are some of the many ways the word is translated in various English versions: rebuking, reproof, convicting of sin, pointing out errors, showing people what is wrong with their lives. I.e., Scripture is intended to identify sins and Satanic lies, and to bring us under conviction for believing these false doctrines and for engaging in sinful behavior.

Third, Scripture is profitable for *epanorthōsis*, another Greek word used just once in the New Testament. This follows up on the previous use of Scripture, which is to identify the sins and errors in our lives. This next word says that the function of Scripture is also to *correct* those sins and errors. Most versions of the New Testament translate it either as "correction" or "correcting." Other versions say Scripture's purpose is straightening us out, improving us, setting us aright, reformation, or restoration. The word shows us what truths we are to substitute for our errors, and what righteous deeds we are to put in place of our sins.

The fourth and final purpose of Scripture listed here is training or instruction in righteousness. This overlaps the general teaching and the corrective functions explained above. For us human beings, righteousness most specifically is "satisfying the requirements of God's law." It can be understood here simply as obedience to law, law-keeping, or upright living. Scripture is thus our authoritative handbook on ethical living, or holiness.

In addition to this explanation of 2 Timothy 3:16-17, I will add two other texts that show why we need God's words and why He has given them to us in the Bible. One is John 20:30-31, "Therefore many other signs Jesus also performed in the presence of the disciples, which are not written in this book; but these have been written so that you may believe that Jesus is the Christ, the Son of God; and that believing you may have life in His name." Here we see that the written Word is given not just to communicate God's truth and God's law to us, but to show us His grace as well. It brings us the full story of salvation through Jesus Christ, and shows us how to access that salvation.

To this I will add Paul's point in 1 Timothy 3:14-15, "I am writing these things to you, hoping to come to you before long; but in case I am delayed, *I write* so that you will know how one ought to conduct himself in the household of God, which is the church of the living God, the pillar and support of the truth." This says that God talks to us Christians in the written Word to show us how we as the CHURCH are supposed to live in the world. It is especially important that we function as a lofty "pillar and support of the truth" in the midst of so much worldly error and evil.

When we consider all the above texts about the role of the written Word of God in our lives as the people of God, we can clearly see why Jesus refuted a false view of the Sadducees in His day with these words: "You are mistaken, not understanding the Scriptures nor the power of God" (Matthew 22:29). Jesus cites one Old Testament text to them (Exodus 3:6) and rebukes them by saying, "Have you not read what was spoken to you by God?" (Matthew 22:31-32). We should think of all Scripture this way: SPOKEN TO US – BY GOD!

Before closing this section, I will briefly answer one more question: why is it so important that we have God's final communication to us in *written* form rather than in ongoing oral revelations? Here are three reasons. One, the written Word is in *permanent* form. Once it is written, it can be preserved and passed along from generation to generation, which is exactly what is the case with Scripture.

Two, the written word is *objective* rather than subjective. Once written, it is "out there" so that everyone can have equal access to it. We do not have to depend on anyone's claims to having received a private revelation, nor do we have to worry about anyone (including ourselves) being deceived by false messages from demonic spirits (1 Timothy 4:1; see Matthew 7:21-23).

Three and finally, a canonical body of written words from God is *exclusive*, i.e., it excludes any of the alleged later "revelations" that are often claimed to exist in various religious groups (e.g., the Roman Catholic Church, many cults, and Pentecostal & Charismatic circles). We can use something Paul said in 1 Corinthians 4:6 as a general principle, that we should "learn not to exceed what is written." We can focus on the written Word, the Bible, as God's only personal communication to us in our time.

THESIS FOUR

When God communicates with us in the Bible in human language, He intends for everything He says to have one specific true and right meaning.

This affirmation — that everything the Bible says has one true and right meaning — is a key idea. (Sometimes I call this "one right meaning" the ORM.) Thesis three says that the Bible as the Word of God (indeed, *words* of God — Romans 3:2) is His personal communication with us human beings. I believe that a basic rule of all verbal communication is that we cannot rightly separate a *statement* from its *meaning*. This should be obvious; it should go without saying. Nevertheless, in connection with Biblical interpretation especially, this is often denied. How often have we heard the claim, "There is no one right way to interpret or understand the Bible!" One well-known Restoration Movement figure has said, "We can believe we are right without believing everyone else is wrong." Disciples of Christ scholar William Baird says the Bible is God's wisdom, and it is of course necessary to *interpret* this divine wisdom. "But [what] turns this wisdom into folly is the notion that one particular understanding is true — that man's wisdom is God's" (*The Corinthian Church*, p. 57, Abingdon 1964).

There is no more subtle yet more destructive attack on the Bible than this. A statement, whether in the Bible or any other writing, is not just a bunch of squiggles on paper. The actual form of such "squiggles" can change, depending on what language one is using. But as used for communication, these things called "words," whether pronounced as specific sounds or written as specific marks on paper, are intended to communicate specific ideas from one person to another. Thus a statement — including every statement or sentence in the Bible — IS its one original meaning as intended by its speaker or writer. *A statement IS its meaning* — we cannot separate them. When God says something in or through the Bible, He MEANS one specific thing. Each statement has ORM.

For example, consider the statement, "Jesus Christ is Lord" (e.g., Philippians 2:11). Each word in that statement has a specific meaning, as determined by its historical, cultural, and literary context. "Jesus Christ" is a specific person. "Is" says that his Lordship is his perpetual identity. "Lord" has a specific meaning in Greek culture and Biblical usage. We have to work to understand all these meanings; but as God (through Paul) made this statement, it has only one right meaning. It is not open to different, exclusive interpretations that are equally valid. One can ask "what it means to me," but only after determining the one right meaning that was in the mind of God when he made the statement. The statement means what God intended it to mean when it first came from the inspired mind of Paul the Apostle and was transferred to us in writing.

Anyone who denies that there is just *one right meaning* for Biblical statements is faced with three serious problems. First, such a position denies the very nature and purpose of language. By its very nature, language is meant to convey specific ideas. Without the ORM (one right meaning) character of language, we may as well keep silent. The pages of the Bible (and all other books) may as well be blank.

This point is well expressed by the Apostle Paul in 1 Corinthians 14, where he explains the difference between the two spiritual gifts of prophecy and speaking in tongues. He explains that when someone speaks in an unknown tongue or language, no one knows the content or meaning of what is being said. In New Testament times such tongue-speaking had sign (evidential) value, but it did not communicate any meaning — unless it was accompanied by the gift of interpretation. But this only proves the point Paul is making.

If the language cannot be understood, it has no value for communication, as Paul says in 1 Corinthians 14:9: "So also you, unless you utter by the tongue speech that is clear, how will it be known what is spoken? For you will be speaking into the air." The gift of prophecy, on the other hand, uses the language of those present and thus is much more valuable than tongue-speaking. In fact, it is two thousand times more valuable, as Paul suggests in verses 18-19! What he says here about prophecy applies to all Scripture, since it is all God's prophetic Word (see 2 Peter 1:20-21). If we cannot understand its one intended meaning, it might as well be in an unknown tongue.

It is true, of course, that we finite human beings sometimes err in our use of language; we say things we really do not mean and then must restate our point. But this cannot be true of the all-knowing God, the very Creator of human language! God the all-knowing one has perfect knowledge of every human language, including Hebrew, Aramaic, and Greek; and He knows how to use them logically, clearly, and unambiguously.

Second, denying that Scripture has just one right meaning ultimately destroys the validity of the concept of truth as such. On the natural level, including all ordinary human communication, there is no absolute truth. The inherent limitations of finite human abilities and experiences prevent us from having absolute, perfect knowledge; therefore we cannot make absolutely true statements about any matters of fact. (This is called the "egocentric predicament.") A world without God or apart from God is a world without truth.

But the infinite God, and He alone, does not have these limitations; His Word is absolute truth (see John 17:17). As we have said in Thesis Two above, "Because the Bible is the Word of God, it is TRUE in every statement, assertion, or affirmation that it makes." Thus by its very nature as the inspired Word of the omniscient Creator-God, the Bible is the ONLY source of absolute truth that exists in our world. But that claim is meaningless and useless unless we can follow it up with, "Because the Bible is the Word of God, every statement, assertion, or affirmation that it makes has *one specific meaning*."

If we say, "There is no one right meaning for Biblical words and sentences and teachings," or even if we say, "There is no way that we can *know* what that one right meaning is" — the Bible loses its truth-character. It is no longer possible to look to the Bible for truth. And since it is generally agreed that there is no absolute truth anywhere else, the world would thus be left with either relativism or agnosticism.

We should remember that the Bible's emphasis on and defense of *truth* and *sound doctrine* are overwhelmingly powerful and fervent. And we should remember that the truth of any statement lies not just in its form (a sequence of marks, words, or sounds), but especially in its content or meaning – a true meaning that can be reworded, or paraphrased, or explained in more detail, or translated into other languages while still *meaning the same thing*. The truth lies in *the meaning*. If a statement is allowed to have multiple meanings that are exclusive or contradictory, then its so-called truth is a fiction, a travesty. If we say that a statement can have multiple legitimate "true" meanings, then the source of that "truth" is not in the statement itself but in the reader(s). (If the original author of Scripture Himself tells us that one of its statements has a second meaning, that is his prerogative and privilege; but that would be by far an exception to the rule, and He Himself would identify that other meaning. See, e.g., Matthew 2:17-18.)

The third problem is this: to say that there is no one right way to understand the Bible is an *insult to God* — the very Creator and Master of language, and the ultimate author of the Bible. See Isaiah 55:11, "So will My word be which goes forth from My mouth; it will not return to Me empty, without accomplishing what I desire, and without succeeding in the matter for which I sent it." To deny the ORM is to say that God has failed to accomplish His purpose for the Bible. As my friend John Fewkes says (in an unpublished manuscript), "To say that a passage means 'A' to you, but 'B' to me is to say that God has failed in His mission to provide us an understandable record of His revelation."

THESIS FIVE

God intends and expects us human beings to know and UNDERSTAND the one specific true and right meaning of Scripture.

Not only does the Bible *have* one true and right meaning, but also: God intends and expects us to know it and understand it. I.e., God expects us not only to know what the Bible says, in the sense of being able to read it and quote it. He also expects us to *understand* it in its one right meaning. I believe this is a point that we have not given adequate attention to. We often stress Bible reading and "Bible study," but do we really drive home the idea that God expects us to discern what his word *means*?

Actually, this is an unspoken assumption behind all language: when we speak, we want and expect our hearers to understand the meaning of what we are saying. This is our intention and hope. (If someone objects and tries to question this, they will do so in language that they expect us to understand!)

One objection that is sometimes raised in Christian circles, though, is that the language of the Bible is different from all other language communication, just because it is the Word of God! I.e., any communication from God must be qualitatively different from human beings speaking to one another, because God's mind and thinking are so far above and beyond ours, and because He is the transcendent and infinite Creator. Thus, they claim, we are too puny and too limited to be able to grasp the meaning of anything uttered by the infinite God.

Here is an example of this claim, taken from an article in the *Christian Standard* (11/20/1983): Human beings are "so small, so dull," so ignorant. But that's OK, as long as we recognize it. We can even "speak in praise of ignorance." Remember: "we are saved by grace, not by knowledge." Thus we are "free to be ignorant," and we are free to disagree with one another about what's true or false. We are "free to tolerate dissent," because we are always "speaking distorted words out of…ignorance."

Here is where an appeal to Isaiah 55:8-9 is usually made. Here Yahweh speaks to us: "For my thoughts are not your thoughts, neither are your ways my ways, declares the LORD. For as the heavens are higher than the earth, so are my ways higher than your ways and my thoughts than your thoughts" (ESV). If this is true, how can we hope to understand the transcendent meanings of God's words?

All of this totally misses the point, though. First, it misses the point of Isaiah 55:8-9. It skips over the fact that Isaiah 55:7 explains that the contrast in vv. 8-9 is NOT between man's puny mental abilities versus God's omniscience, but between man's WICKED ways and UNRIGHTEOUS thoughts, versus God's holy and pure ones: "Let the wicked forsake his way and the unrighteous man his thoughts; let him return to the LORD" (ESV).

Second, this misses the very point of God's transcendent, infinite knowledge and abilities. *Just because* he is so exceedingly brilliant and intelligent, he is *able* to adjust his superior verbal communication efforts *to our level*. To use an illustration I saw decades ago in a *Christianity Today* article, God's ability to speak to us on our level is like that of a Nobel prize-winning, Ph.D. physicist who can talk business on the level of Stephen Hawking if he wants to, but can also say to his five-year-old son, "Come on, Johnny, let's go to the park and play ball; then we will get some ice cream!"

The main point here is that we must be careful not to insult God! The Bible may have some material similar to a physicist's lecture to post-graduate students, but it is more like the chat with the child, or at least with ordinary people. Do we not understand that God knows our limits, and that He is brilliant enough to know how to speak to us on our level? Certainly, God expects and intends for us to understand His words! Else why would He have given them to us in the first place? Scripture is where God's mind connects with our minds! We are called on by Scripture itself to believe this.

Here are some Scripture texts that make it clear that God intends for us to *understand* His word. We begin with Hebrews 11:3, "By faith we understand [*noeō*] that the worlds were prepared by the word of God, so that what is seen was not made out of things which are visible." This is an allusion to Genesis 1, with its suggestion of *ex nihilo* creation — certainly not a simple subject. Yet Hebrews says that our minds [*nous*, with which we *noeō*] grasp or understand what God is telling us about creation.

This leads us to Hebrews 4:12, "For the word of God is living and active and sharper than any two-edged sword, and piercing as far as the division of soul and spirit, of both joints and marrow, and able to judge the thoughts and intentions of the heart." In this text the soul, spirit, and heart are different words for the same thing, i.e., the innermost spiritual part of our being, as distinct from the body. The point is that when God speaks to us, His Word is of such a nature that it pierces — goes all the way down — into our innermost self, where it interacts with the thoughts and intentions of our hearts, i.e., with our mind, our intellect, our will. This shows that the very purpose of God's Word is to engage our minds. How can it do this unless we can *understand* it? Connecting with God is not some mystical experience that bypasses our thought processes; it is done through the activity of the mind and understanding.

In Matthew 22:37 Jesus says, "You shall love the Lord your God with all your heart, and with all your soul, and with all your mind." (Luke 10:27 is very similar.) As in Hebrews 4:12, here the words heart, soul, and mind are referring to the "inner man" (Ephesians 3:16) in all its aspects. The command is to love God from within, including with our MIND. The Greek word for "mind" is *dianoia*, which stands for our "understanding, intelligence, or mind." Mark 12:33 uses a synonymous word, *sunesis*, which specifically means "understanding or intelligence." Thus we are COMMANDED to love God with our UNDERSTANDING!

Here is another text that refers to our responsibility to understand God's Word, namely, 2 Corinthians 1:13-14, "For we write nothing else to you than what you read and understand, and I hope you will understand until the end, just as you also partially did understand us." Here we must note that Paul expects his readers not only to *read* what he writes, but also to *understand* it. The Greek word is *epiginōskō*, which Paul uses three times. It is a strong word for "to know, to understand."

Here in verse 13 Paul says his hope is that his readers will understand his message "until the end," as the NASB puts it. Many take this phrase, *heōs telous*, to mean "up to the end of time." However, the contrast with *apo merous* ("in part," translated "partially"), shows that *heōs telous* means something like "up to the highest degree, completely." Thus Paul is saying here that his readers thus far have only partially understood him, but his hope and desire is that they will ultimately understand him completely, i.e., *in the way that he intended*. The word *telous* is the genitive form of *telos*, one meaning of which is "goal, aim, purpose, intention." I.e., the latter part of v. 13 should be read, "I hope you will understand what I am writing in the way I intend it to be understood." Keep working on it until you get the ORM.

Finally, in Colossians 1:9-10 Paul prays that his readers "may be filled with the knowledge of His will in all spiritual wisdom and understanding [*sunesis*]," so that we may be "increasing in the knowledge of God." This is the same word for "understanding" that is used in Mark 12:33, *sunesis* (see above). Note also that Paul says he prays that we may be FILLED with the knowledge of God's will in ALL wisdom and understanding. Here again the goal is not just a half-way or garbled or tentative understanding, but one that goes all the way.

These texts are clear enough, and they show the truth of this fifth thesis, that God intends and expects us to know and *understand* the one right meaning of His word. Actually, the very fact that He has spoken to us at all should establish this. Why would God speak to us, if He did not expect and intend for us to understand what He has said?

The problem here is that the Christian world has obviously fallen so far short of this goal that it is difficult to take the Biblical teaching about it seriously. It seems so unlikely or even impossible to achieve such a goal, given the dominant lack of agreement among Christians as to the meaning of Scripture. How can we hope to find that one right meaning of Biblical texts, and especially in a way that we can agree on what that one right meaning is? It just seems easier to pretend that such a responsibility and such a goal do not exist.

For those who may feel that this is an unmanageable burden, I will now point out some other Biblical teachings that will help to make this burden lighter. First, discerning the ORM of Scripture is likely to be a long process, similar to (indeed, as a part of) sanctification. It will not happen all at once. This is seen in the discussion of 2 Corinthians 1:13-14, above. Paul described the Corinthian Christians' understanding at that time as being *apo merous*, or "partial." They still needed to pursue it to its fullness, *heōs telous*.

The pursuit of this goal is the process that 2 Peter 3:18 describes as growing in grace and knowledge. We begin the process by humbling ourselves as children (Matthew 18:4; 19:14), even being "like newborn babies" who "long for the pure milk of the word" (1 Peter 2:2). But we are expected to grow and mature, especially in our understanding of the faith: "Brethren, do not be children in your thinking; yet in evil be infants, but in your thinking be mature" (1 Corinthians 14:20). This is the "growing in knowledge" of which 2 Peter 3:18 speaks. Those who ignore their responsibility to mature in their understanding are severely rebuked in Hebrews 5:11-6:3. They are compared to infants who continue to suckle milk when they should be eating solid food (5:12). If we are not chewing on the solid meat of the Word, we cannot expect to grow and mature

(5:13-14). So "let us press on to maturity" (6:1) by advancing into some of the more difficult parts of Scripture (6:2-3).

Second, we must simply recognize that some parts of Scripture are indeed harder to understand than others. The Apostle Peter reminds us of this when in 2 Peter 3:16 he refers to Paul's letters, "in which are some things hard to understand, which the untaught and unstable distort, as they do also in the rest of the Scriptures, to their own destruction." People who heard Jesus teach sometimes had difficulty understanding Him. E.g., when Jesus taught about eating His flesh and drinking His blood (John 6:52-58), many of His disciples said, "This is a difficult statement; who can listen to it?" (John 6:60). Also, many Old Testament prophecies of the first coming of Jesus were by their very nature unable to be understood by believers under the Old Covenant, even by their human authors. But we can understand them now, as they are explained by the New Testament writers (1 Peter 1:10-12).

Thus we are not alone today when we struggle to understand some teachings of the Word, e.g., concerning events of the *second* coming of Jesus, especially in the apocalyptic literature of the Book of Revelation. This does not, however, give us an excuse for being discouraged and giving up in our efforts to understand God's Word. It simply means that we must be patient as we continue to pursue the *heōs telous* goal of finding the Bible's one true meaning. Finding that meaning will be harder and take longer regarding some parts of Scripture than others.

Finally, though all are expected to understand the Bible's teaching, God does not expect every Christian to have the same level of ability to discern and formulate the one right understanding. This is why some Christians are spiritually gifted to be *teachers*. These are the ones who have, by God's gift, the special ability to understand and explain the Word. Jesus's own example shows us both the need for such teachers, and specifically what their task is meant to be. Throughout His ministry He explained Old Testament Scriptures, e.g. concerning John the Baptist

(Matthew 11:10), concerning His own mission (Luke 4:17-21), and His betrayal by Judas (John 13:18).

Jesus's example as a teacher explaining Scripture is seen especially in how He taught His disciples the meaning of His death and resurrection. After His resurrection, the disciples were puzzled by events on resurrection morning, "for as yet they did not understand the Scripture, that He must rise again from the dead" (John 20:9). An example of this lack of understanding is the two on the road to Emmaus: they just did not get it (see Luke 24:13-24)! Jesus told them that their problem was a lack of understanding of Scripture! See Luke 24:25, "O foolish men and slow of heart to believe in all that the prophets have spoken!" Then (v. 27), "beginning with Moses and with all the prophets, He explained to them the things concerning Himself in all the Scriptures." i.e., he explained to them *the one true meaning of Scripture*!

See then what Jesus later said to his gathered disciples in Luke 24:44-46, where "He opened their minds to understand the Scriptures" (v. 45)! He opened their minds through teaching, not through some miracle, so that they could *understand* the one true meaning of Scripture.

In the early church, between Christ's return to the Father and the completion of the New Testament canon, God provided Holy Spirit-inspired teachers to receive new revelation and present new inspired teaching to His people. These were the prophets and apostles of Ephesians 3:5 and 4:11. He also began, and continues, to provide uninspired but Spirit-*enabled* teachers who have the special task and ability to teach the meaning of God's Word to God's people. We see this spiritual gift named in Romans 12:7; 1 Corinthians 12:28-29; and Ephesians 4:11. Such teachers are not infallible and will not know everything, but their work is crucial. They must perform their teaching task conscientiously and take it very seriously (see James 3:1).

This teaching ministry especially applies to elders (1 Timothy 3:2; 5:17; Titus 1:9) and evangelists (2 Timothy 2:24), both of whom are required to be *didaktikon*, a Greek word translated "able to teach." Those who are teachers have a responsibility to be good stewards of their gift, and others in the congregation have a responsibility to let themselves be fed by the fruit of their labor.

All of the above shows that coming to the one right understanding of Scripture is not necessarily something that will happen immediately and easily, but it also shows us just how strongly God wants and intends for us to come to that one right understanding of the Word He has communicated to us. And here I will add one more point that shows just how important this is to God, namely, the emphasis that He puts on the EVIL of false teaching and false teachers in the New Testament Scriptures.

First, we should notice how harshly Jesus warned against false teachers. "Beware of the false prophets, who come to you in sheep's clothing, but inwardly are ravenous wolves" (Matthew 7:15). To the Pharisees and scribes He said, "You hypocrites …teaching as doctrines the precepts of men" (Matthew 15:7-9). Another warning: "See to it that no one misleads you" (Matthew 24:4), for "many false prophets will arise and will mislead many" (Matthew 24:11). "False Christs and false prophets will arise and will show great signs and wonders, so as to mislead" (Matthew 24:24). "Woe to you lawyers! For you have taken away the key of knowledge; you yourselves did not enter, and you hindered those who were entering" (Luke 11:52).

Here is Paul's strong instruction to the elders of the church at Ephesus: "Be on guard for yourselves and for all the flock, among which the Holy Spirit has made you overseers, to shepherd the church of God which He purchased with His own blood. I know that after my departure savage wolves will come in among you, not sparing the flock; and from among your own selves men will arise, speaking perverse things, to draw away the disciples after them."

In his Pastoral Epistles (to Timothy and Titus) Paul continues this kind of warning. In 1 Timothy 1:3 he tells Timothy to command certain men at Ephesus "not to teach strange doctrines." In 1 Timothy 4:1 he says that "in later times some will fall away from the faith, paying attention to deceitful spirits and doctrines of demons." He continues in vv. 2-3, saying that we can resist such hypocritical liars by believing and knowing the truth. Anyone who "advocates a different doctrine and does not agree with sound words …is conceited and understands nothing" (1 Timothy 6:3-4). Timothy is specifically warned to avoid false teaching based on "what is falsely called 'knowledge'" (1 Timothy 6:20).

Paul continues such cautions in his second letter to Timothy. He tells Timothy to have nothing to do with "foolish and ignorant speculations," and to correct those who teach such (2 Timothy 2:23, 25). Titus likewise is told to instruct elders to believe and teach sound doctrine, and to *refute* those who teach otherwise (Titus 1:9). Titus is told that "empty talkers and deceivers … must be silenced," and that he must "reprove them severely so that they may be sound in the faith" (Titus 1:10-13).

Hebrews 13:9 utters this command: "Do not be carried away by varied and strange teachings."

In his second letter, the Apostle Peter condemns false prophets and false teachers who introduce destructive heresies and blaspheme the way of truth (2 Peter 2:1-2). These false teachers are like animals who do not know how to use their minds, and have no real knowledge (2:12). They revel in their deceptions; they forsake the right way; they speak empty, boastful words (2:13, 15, 18). Peter warns us not be let ourselves be carried away by the error of these lawless ones (3:17).

In his letters the Apostle John continues this same theme. He warns us not to believe every spirit, since many false prophets have gone out into the world (1 John 4:1). We must know how to distinguish "the spirit of truth" from "the spirit of error" (4:6), because "many deceivers have gone out into the world" (2 John 7).

These many warnings against false teaching just re-emphasize the main point of this section, that we cannot be too serious about the need to understand the one right meaning of Scripture. The distinction between truth and falsehood is a life-and-death matter. God expects us to understand His Word.

At this point someone might raise the question, is this expecting *too much* of us mere mortals? The answer is NO, and the reason for this answer will be seen in the next thesis.

THESIS SIX

We CAN understand this one true and right meaning of Scripture, because we have been created in the image of God.

We are asserting here not only that Scripture HAS one right meaning which we human beings are expected to understand, but also that we human beings actually CAN understand that one right meaning. But the question here is this: how do we KNOW that we have this ability to understand the Bible? So far we have suggested that this is implied by the following three points: (1) the very nature of human language; (2) the omniscient God as the origin of Scripture; and (3) the Bible's own emphasis on truth and sound doctrine, along with its many warnings against false doctrine.

But there is one more main fact that establishes our conclusion that we CAN discern the one right meaning of Scripture, namely, that we have been *created in the image of God*. This is how we know that God intends and expects us to understand His communication addressed to us, *and* that we are able to do so: He *made us for this very purpose!* From the very beginning, human beings have been equipped to receive and understand God's words.

In the very first chapter of the Bible (Genesis 1:26-27), we read, "Then God said, 'Let Us make man in Our image, according to Our likeness.'" Then it happened: "God created man in His own image, in the image of God He created him; male and female He created them." This fact is simply assumed throughout the rest of the Bible, with little or no explanation or discussion. It is mentioned only twice more in the Old Testament (Genesis 5:1; 9:1-6) and twice in the New Testament (1 Corinthians 11:7; James 3:9). Our knowledge of its content is actually understood from two passages which discuss salvation as being RE-created in God's image; these will be discussed below.

From all of these texts together, we do know the basic nature of the image of God within us. We know that our likeness to God is built into our *spiritual* essence, not our physical bodies. (We know this because God is not composed of physical stuff.) In Scripture our spiritual essence is spoken of as our spirit, our soul, our heart, and our inner man. It includes the following spiritual abilities: (1) Intellectual (logical, reasoning) abilities, through what we call the MIND. (2) Volitional, decision-making powers, through our WILL. (3) Our MORAL sense, the consciousness of right and wrong. (4) EMOTIONAL experiences, i.e., feelings and affections.

Animals may have most of these abilities to some extent, but their natures are qualitatively different from human beings because, of all earthly creatures, only we human beings have spirits that are made in God's image, and thus have this one unique quality which embraces all of the above: PERSONHOOD. Human beings are *persons*, personal beings, with personal identity patterned after the personal nature of God (who is the three persons of the Trinity). This *personhood* is the key, unique, distinguishing feature of the image of God. What makes us unique as persons is a unique capacity or ability to *know God*, to consciously *relate to God*, to *love and worship God*, to have *fellowship with God*, and finally, to actually *communicate with God* in a common language.

This last point is very important. We have noted earlier that the Trinitarian nature of God means that the three persons of the Trinity have existed forever in a relationship of communion and communication with one another. See, for example, Genesis 1:26, "Let Us make man in Our image"; Genesis 3:22, "Behold, the man has become like one of Us"; Genesis 11:7, "Come, let Us go down and there confuse their language."

Here we see the persons of the Trinity communicating among themselves. And God made us in His image because He wants to communicate *with us!* We have been given our rational and volitional abilities especially for this purpose. God speaks to us on our level; and by our created, image-bearing nature we are able to understand him. That is what the image of God is all about.

How do we know that the essence of the image of God includes this ability to know and communicate intelligibly with God? As mentioned above, we know this because of what Paul says about the *re*-creation of the image of God that is part of our salvation package. We are told that being saved from sin includes a working of God that is like being re-created or created anew. The implication is that sin has damaged the image of God within us, and it needs to be repaired or restored. God begins this process in our baptism, when we receive the "regeneration and renewing by the Holy Spirit" (Titus 3:5). As a result, "if anyone is in Christ, he is a new creature" (2 Corinthians 5:17). "We are His workmanship, created in Christ Jesus for good works" (Ephesians 2:10).

This act of re-creation is specifically aimed at correcting the damage done to the image of God within us. We know this because of the way Paul describes it in the parallel texts of Ephesians 4:23-24 and Colossians 3:9-10. Here Paul speaks not only of the beginning point of this new creation (our regeneration, new birth, spiritual resurrection in baptism), but also of its ongoing expansion (our progressive sanctification). In the Colossians text he specifically says this is a renewing of the image originally given us by the Creator.

I will now quote the passages, beginning with Ephesians 4:23-24, where Paul urges us to pursue what God began in us in our baptism. He says that you must "be renewed in the spirit of your mind, and put on the new self, which in the likeness of God has been created in righteousness and holiness of the truth." In Colossians 3:9-10 he speaks of it more as what God has already accomplished in the regeneration event, as he urges us not to sin, "since you laid aside the old self with its evil practices, and have put on the new self who is being renewed to a true knowledge according to the image of the One who created him."

From these texts we learn the nature of the original image of God, the damage done to that image by sin, and what is involved in the salvific restoration of the image. Without going into detail, we can say that the language in these texts states that the image is being renewed unto "righteousness and holiness of the truth" (Ephesians). This reference to "righteousness and holiness" shows that there is a moral aspect to the image of God. In the beginning, Adam and Eve were morally pure and without sin; they were righteous and holy. Sin corrupted this holy state, but redemption is restoring it.

More specifically, Paul says the image is being renewed unto "the holiness *of truth*" (Ephesians) and to "true knowledge" (Colossians). Some versions translate the Ephesians statement as "true holiness," but that is not how it reads in the Greek. The Greek text literally says we are being re-created "in holiness of the truth." These references to truth and knowledge show that there is an epistemological or intellectual aspect to the image of God. Our first parents had not only some innate, built-in knowledge, but also a built-in *ability* to think, to reason, to use logic and evidence, and to use language. Sin corrupted this, but the re-creation of the image of God is renewing our ability to use our minds as God intended. This redemptive work affects not only *what* we think but also *how* we think — not only the contents of our minds, but also the very process of right thinking as well as our attitude toward the truth.

The phrase Paul uses in Ephesians 4:24 – "holiness of the truth" – shows that there is a MORAL aspect to the way we use our minds, i.e., it is a matter of right or wrong. This applies in several ways. First, it applies to HOW we use our minds. There is a right and holy way to use our minds, and there is a wrong and sinful way to think. Morality applies to epistemology. We are morally obligated to use proper logic and reasoning, and to follow the rules of evidence — especially when we are engaged in the process of establishing *truth*. We have a moral responsibility to use our minds properly, and to avoid logical fallacies and hermeneutical errors. This is important because it is directly related to the task of understanding the one right meaning of God's communication with us in Scripture. Our intellectual ability to do this is part of what it means to be created — indeed, RE-created — in the image of God.

In the second place, the morality (i.e., holiness) of truth also includes making every effort to prevent our WILL from interfering with and overruling our intellect, especially when we are trying to understand Scripture. The dominance of the will over the intellect in the fallen world is seen in Romans 1:18-25, where Paul shows how the pagan world deliberately suppresses the truth in order to justify their unrighteousness (v. 18). Professing to be wise, they become fools (v. 22), and exchange the truth of God for a lie (v. 25). Ephesians 4:18 sums this up by saying that they are "darkened in their understanding" (i.e., the intellect) because of "the hardness of their heart" (i.e., the will). See also Paul's figurative use of the "veil" in 2 Corinthians 3:14-18. He applies this to the Jews who refused to see the truth about Jesus in the Old Testament Scriptures. (See also 2 Corinthians 4:3-4.)

This is one of the main effects of sin upon us: it causes our will to control our intellect, so that the desires of the will lead us to suppress the rules of hermeneutics and find in Scripture what we WANT to find there, regardless of how intelligent we may be. This is why we need the power of the indwelling Holy Spirit, i.e., to restore within us the holiness of the truth by enabling us to think clearly as we are trying to understand Scripture.

This leads to the final aspect of the holiness of the truth that is being restored within us, i.e., we are being enabled to do what we OUGHT to be doing about truth. Through the restoration of the image of God within us, we are now able to (1) *know* the truth. Jesus said, "And you will know the truth, and the truth will make you free" (John 8:32). In 2 John 1, the Beloved Apostle refers to "all who know the truth." Knowing the truth, and separating it from falsehood, is where "holiness of the truth" begins.

This leads to the second thing we ought to do, i.e., not just know the truth but also to (2) *believe* the truth. This is crucial, because God will make sure that "all may be judged who did not believe the truth" (2 Thessalonians 2:12). Knowing and believing the truth must be supplemented by (3) *loving* the truth. This too is crucial, because those who allow themselves to be deceived will perish, "because they did not receive the love of the truth so as to be saved" (2 Thessalonians 2:10). Finally, the holiness of the truth leads us to (4) *speak* the truth, in love, because this is part of what it means to "grow up" to maturity through the restoration of the image of God within us (Ephesians 4:13, 15).

Being re-made in God's image is another way of describing the second part of the double cure of salvation, i.e., our regeneration event in baptism, followed by the lifelong process of sanctification. The way Paul describes the restoring of this image shows that the Holy Spirit's sanctifying work is not just giving us the power to obey God's commands, but also includes the restoring of our cognitive ability to have *true knowledge* of God and of whatever He decides to communicate to us. I.e., our sanctification includes not only *doing RIGHT things* (i.e., righteousness), but also *knowing, understanding, and believing TRUE things* (i.e., holiness of the truth). I take the latter to include the ability and effort to understand the one right meaning of God's Word. Having a true understanding of God's words is part of what it means to be holy as God is holy (1 Peter 1:15-16).

As is true of sanctification in general, being re-made in God's image does not mean that we become morally perfect immediately, or that we all at once will have perfect understanding of the meaning of Scripture and of everything else. We are in the process of *growing* in grace and knowledge (2 Peter 3:18); we are getting better and better at it. The more we grow and learn, the better we become at learning more.

Because we are still morally imperfect, though, we will still have flaws in our behavior and in our thinking processes. Also, because our knowledge is finite and not omniscient, we will still have some uncertainty about specific Scriptures and will be subject to errors in understanding. And even in the things we do understand, our finiteness means we will never have absolute (100%) certainty about what we believe is right and true. What we can have, and do have, however, is *moral* certainty. This is our goal. It is God's intention for us, and it is *possible* because we are made — and are being RE-made — in the image of God!

Certain knowledge and certain truth can come only from the mind of the omniscient God, the One who created us in His image and who speaks to us in His Word. Our ability and responsibility to understand His Word are part of the very reason why He made us in His image. It is probably beyond our ability to grasp just how amazing, how awesome, how astounding it is that the transcendent, infinite GOD actually speaks to us, and that we can *understand what He says!* But this is the very point of being created — and *re*-created — in His image!

THESIS SEVEN

We as human beings not only CAN understand the one true and right meaning of Scripture; we are under MORAL OBLIGATION to do so, i.e., NOT to understand the one true meaning of Scripture is a sin.

This is a crucial, pivotal point in this list of theses: we are under *moral obligation* to discern and understand the one right meaning of Biblical statements. This is already strongly implied by theses five and six above, that God intends and expects us to understand His Word, and has equipped and enabled us to do so in the way He has made us and saved us. Here, however, we see that there is no ambiguity or doubt about this obligation, because we are actually instructed and commanded to understand it.

Here is the point: we must not only read the Bible and know (be aware of) what it teaches; we must also understand it in its one right meaning. This is not just something *optional* that we are free either to pursue or not to pursue. We are commanded to do this; it is a key part of our required sanctification.

Based on my lifetime of experience as a church worker, I must say that we Christian people have never really recognized or acknowledged this obligation. We work hard to evangelize and convert sinners, and we welcome them into the church. But what do we actually require of them as new Christians? We let them know that God expects them to be active in the church by attending maybe once a week for worship and fellowship; we show them that they must participate in the Lord's Supper, in giving, in prayer, and in Bible reading. We expect them to change their lifestyles where necessary.

But what do we really expect and require of them regarding the Word of God? We teach them to know and believe it truly IS the Word of God, and we encourage them to *read* their Bibles and listen to one sermon a week that may or may not explain something the Bible teaches. Some churches still provide optional Sunday School classes for group Bible study; but as a rule we do not *require* our members to attend, and the percent who do attend has become disappointingly low. And for those who do attend, what material do they study?

In my judgment we have a huge vacuum here in our nurturing of Christians. Are we making sure that our people are acquiring an accurate knowledge of the one right meaning of the Word of God? Or are we implying that Bible study is optional, and that everyone is free — has the "right" — to come to his or her own understanding of what the Bible means? Even raising such questions as this will sound crazy to many people. But we have already seen in the previous six theses that *there is one right meaning of the Bible's teaching*. Now we are simply trying to answer the "So what?" question.

I am absolutely serious about this — that every Christian needs to know that the Bible has ONE RIGHT MEANING, and that this puts us under the spiritual obligation *to understand that one right meaning of the Word of God*. It is part of our New Covenant law code. It is not just a "do it if you want to" or "do it if you have time" project. It is a *command*, a moral obligation, an OUGHT, a "holiness of the truth" issue. If the Bible is truly the Word of God, these obligations naturally follow:

1. We ought to *believe* everything the Bible says is true.

2. We ought to *obey* every command that applies to us in this New Covenant era.

3. We ought to come to a *correct understanding* of the *meaning* of the Bible's statements and commands.

What follows here is an explanation of a few texts that lay this last obligation upon us.

Where does the Bible say we have an obligation to understand it? We will start with Jesus's parable of the sower and his seed in Matthew 13:1-9.

> [1] That day Jesus went out of the house and was sitting by the sea. [2] And large crowds gathered to Him, so He got into a boat and sat down, and the whole crowd was standing on the beach. [3] And He spoke many things to them in parables, saying, "Behold, the sower went out to sow; [4] and as he sowed, some seeds fell beside the road, and the birds came and ate them up. [5] Others fell on the rocky places, where they did not have much soil; and immediately they sprang up, because they had no depth of soil. [6] But when the sun had risen, they were scorched; and because they had no root, they withered away. [7] Others fell among the thorns, and the thorns came up and choked them out. [8] And others fell on the good soil and yielded a crop, some a hundredfold, some sixty, and some thirty. [9] He who has ears, let him hear."

See also Mark's version of this parable in Mark 4:2-9, and Luke's summary of it in Luke 8:4-8. Luke points out that Jesus added this explanation: "The seed is the word of God" (Luke 8:11).

In the discussion that follows the telling of the parable, as recorded in Matthew 13:10ff., Jesus shows us that simply reading the Word is not enough. In 13:13 Jesus distinguishes seeing, hearing, and understanding the Word. Speaking of those who fail on each point, he says, "While seeing they do not see, and while hearing they do not hear, nor do they understand." In verses 14-15 he relates this to a quotation from Isaiah 6:9-10 that speaks of unbelieving Israelites, "You will keep on hearing, but will not understand; you will keep on seeing, but will not perceive." Also, "They have closed their eyes, otherwise they would see with their eyes, hear with their ears, and understand with their heart."

Continuing to explain the parable, in 13:19 Jesus says of the seed that fell beside the road and was eaten by birds (v. 4): "When anyone hears the word of the kingdom and does not understand it, the evil one comes and snatches away what has been sown in his heart." In 13:23, explaining the seed that fell on good soil (v. 8), Jesus says, "And the one on whom seed was sown on the good soil, this is the man who hears the word and understands it."

As we can see, over and over in this discussion, Jesus specifies the necessity of *understanding* the Word. Reading and hearing it are not enough. No wonder he rebukes his Jewish followers on another occasion with these words: "Why do you not understand what I am saying?" (John 8:43).

On another occasion, when Jesus was teaching the crowd of people that followed Him, Matthew 15:10 says, "After Jesus called the crowd to Him, He said to them, 'Hear and understand.'" This is a direct commandment to understand the one right meaning of what Jesus was about to teach them.

In Romans 3:9-18 the Apostle Paul cites fourteen Old Testament passages that emphasize the sinfulness of all human beings: "There is none righteous, not even one" (3:10); "there is none who does good, there is not even one" (3:12). In this list of indictments, the second one named as an aspect of human sinfulness is this: "There is none who understands" (from Psalm 14:2; 53:2). The point here is that Paul names *failure to understand God's words and ways as a SIN!*

In the midst of teaching us various instructions from the New Covenant law code, in Ephesians 5:17 the Apostle Paul says, "So then do not be foolish, but understand what the will of the Lord is." The Greek word translated "foolish" is *aphrōn*, which does mean "foolish" or "ignorant." (See its use in Luke 11:40; 12:20; Romans 2:20; 1 Peter 2:15.) This word comes from the common Greek word *phroneō*, which means "to think, to use your mind, to come to a judgment about something." With the negating alpha added at the front ("*a-*") it means the opposite: "*not* thinking, *not* using your mind, *not* coming to the right conclusion." So what is the solution? Paul says it very clearly: "But UNDERSTAND what the will of the Lord is"! We are *commanded* to *understand*!

In one other text from Paul's writings, the Apostle addresses Timothy in 2 Timothy 2:15 thus: "Be diligent to present yourself approved to God as a workman who does not need to be ashamed, accurately handling the word of truth." The key English expression here is "accurately handling." We often hear it translated, "rightly dividing" (e.g., KJV, NKJV), as if we are being exhorted to properly distinguish the Old Covenant from the New Covenant.

Such a proper division of the Word is necessary, but this is not the point of this text. The Greek word here is *orthotomeō*, from two other Greek words, *orthos*, "straight, correct" (as in "orthodox"); and *tomos*, "sharp for cutting." The idea is this: when you are studying and teaching the Word of God, cut straight to the point! *Find that One Right Meaning and lay it bare*! Here are a few versions of the New Testament that get the point: "correctly teaching" (*Christian Standard Bible*); "teaching accurately" (NET Bible®); "correctly explains" (*New Living Translation*); "rightly explaining" (*New Revised Standard Version*).

This teaching of the one right meaning is in contrast with the false teachers condemned in 2 Timothy 3:1ff., who are "always learning and never able to come to the knowledge of the truth" (3:7). Such false teachers remind me of professors who think their job is just to rehearse the possible views on a subject and let the students come to their own conclusions — or who say that their job is to teach learners *how* to think, and not *what* to think (which is a fine example of the fallacy of false choice).

Ceslas Spicq, in his very useful *Theological Lexicon of the New Testament* (Hendrickson 1994, II:595), says the Greeks used this word — *orthotomeō* — to mean "to cut a path in a straight direction." So when Paul uses this word, says Spicq, it "is diametrically opposed to distortions and falsifications of the Word of God (2 Cor 2:17; 4:2) by bad exegetes who twist texts (2 Peter 3:16)."

These are the key texts that establish for us the obligation to study the Bible until we have come to the correct understanding of it, until we have discerned its *one right meaning*.

Before leaving this section I will present one more category of texts that establish this same moral obligation, but from a different direction. These are texts that tell us that believing *false doctrine*, which includes *wrong understandings* of God's Word, is the result of Satanic deception and is SINFUL. We are strongly warned against believing and teaching false doctrine, including false, incorrect understandings of Biblical texts.

We begin with Paul's warning to the Corinthian Christians in 2 Corinthians 11:3, "But I am afraid that, as the serpent deceived Eve by his craftiness, your minds will be led astray from the simplicity and purity of *devotion* to Christ." Exactly how did the serpent deceive Eve? According to Genesis 3:1-6, he did so by presenting to her a false interpretation of God's words, earlier spoken to Adam (Genesis 2:15-17). Paul is exhorting us here not to let Satan mess with our minds. The Greek word for "minds" is *noēma*, meaning "mind, thought, the contents of the mind, the way we think." Paul uses the same word in 2 Corinthians 2:11 to refer to Satan's mind or thoughts. What better way for the devil to deceive us than to allow us to accept the Bible as God's Word but to tempt us to interpret it falsely? And how would he do this? Through false teachers who themselves are deceived by their phony "angel of light" (2 Corinthians 11:13-15). Paul is warning us to be on guard against such deceivers.

Looking again at 1 Timothy 4:1ff., we remember that we are warned that "some will fall away from the faith, paying attention to deceitful spirits and doctrines of demons" (v. 1). We can avoid this by making sure we continue to be "nourished on the words of the faith and of the sound doctrine which you have been following" (v. 6). We will remember also that the Apostle John connects false teachings with demonic spirits (1 John 4:1, 6).

Here is one other text that relates the believing and teaching of false doctrine to Satanic deception, namely, 2 Timothy 2:25-26, where Paul urges Timothy to gently correct those who are opposing him by spreading false teachings, "if perhaps God may grant them repentance leading to the knowledge of the truth, and they may come to their senses *and escape* from the snare of the devil, having been held captive by him to do his will." Those guilty of this sin included Hymenaeus and Philetus, whose "worldly and empty chatter" was beginning to "spread like gangrene" (vv. 16-17). They were guilty of having "gone astray from the truth" and of teaching "foolish and ignorant speculations" (vv. 18, 23). Paul's description of their sinful condition is terrifying, as he indicates that they are caught in "the snare of the devil, having been held captive by him to do his will" (v. 26).

All of this indicates how crucial it is that we get serious about our moral obligation to embrace with our minds the truth of God's Word according to its one true and right meaning. Not to do so is a sin of the mind, a sin that requires repentance and a subsequent effort to seek "the knowledge of the truth" (2 Timothy 2:25). James 5:19-20 says that one who "strays from the truth" is a "sinner" who needs to be turned "from the error of his way." Here is our moral imperative: "Do not be carried away by varied and strange teachings" (Hebrews 13:9). As Paul says in Ephesians 5:6, "Let no one deceive you with empty words, for because of these things the wrath of God comes upon the sons of disobedience."

THESIS EIGHT

We must not only understand and believe the one true and right meaning of Scripture; we must actually HOLD FAST to this understanding with full assurance, confidence, and conviction.

This thesis is not about *what* we must do, but *how* we must do it. Yes, the Bible commands us to understand the one true and right meaning of Scripture, and it goes even further than this. It also commands us to do so with an attitude or a sense of certitude and conviction. It is always proper to say things like "This seems to be the best view," or "In my best judgment," or "As I understand it"; but such qualifiers should never be meant to convey doubt or uncertainty about what we are teaching. We must not just "hold to" the positions we take on the meaning of Scripture; we should "hold FAST to" them.

In our culture this is not the accepted view. Today, having strong convictions that you are right and that those who disagree with you are wrong is seen as a flaw in your character: the sin of arrogance. Many in the Restoration Movement are following this path. They (dogmatically!) tell us it is arrogant, dogmatic, and Pharisaical to want to be certain about what you believe. For example, an article in *Christian Standard* called "The Culture of Certainty" (May 2017) says, in summary, that it is better to suspect that you might be wrong about something than to be convinced you are right about it. The author calls it "humility" and "maturity" to know that you are bound to be wrong about something, but have no idea what that might be. "We do not need one more inflexible, myopic ideologue. We need more people willing to face the reality that they may be wrong."

I certainly (!) grant that our finiteness means it is always possible to be wrong. But in light of Scripture I must say that this is not intended to be the norm! CERTAINTY is the intended norm! According to the Bible our problem is not "the culture of certainty," but *the peril of uncertainty*, where we are under the influence of weenies who are afraid to say, "I know this is true! I know this is right!"

We have too many progressive, trendy new-thinkers who want to substitute *relativism* for certainty, and *Christian agnosticism* for Christian conviction. They want to cram as much as possible into the category of "opinion." The problem is that they are confusing "moral certainty" with "100% philosophical certainty." I believe it is true that it is not possible for us finite creatures to have 100% technical certainty regarding matters of fact. Only the omniscient God has this kind of certainty.

But we must remember that we are created in the image of God. A main part of that image is the ability to use logic and reason and evidence, and thus the ability to reach conclusions that are beyond reasonable doubt — indeed, beyond moral doubt. Doubt is morally acceptable where evidence is lacking or is weak in comparison with evidence to the contrary. But we cannot deny that our God-given rational and logical abilities are able to determine when the evidence establishes something to be true. When this happens we have moral certainty. This moral certainty is a state of mind where we recognize that the evidence for something is so solid that it is immoral — sinful — to doubt or deny it. This is part of "the holiness of truth" (Ephesians 4:24).

Such moral certainty is an attitude or state of mind, not a logical or metaphysical technicality. We already know that this concept of moral certainty applies to knowing that we are saved; thus we speak of having "assurance of salvation." Now we are saying that this also applies to our understanding of the Word of God: we are supposed to have "assurance of understanding."

The Bible teaches us this, according to the following relevant texts. First, in 1 Corinthians 11:2 Paul praises the Corinthians for *holding firmly* to what he had taught them, just as they had been taught. He says, "Now I praise you because you remember me in everything and hold firmly to the traditions, just as I delivered them to you." Also, he tells the Christians at Philippi that he wants to hear that they "are standing firm in one spirit, with one mind, striving together for the faith of the gospel" (Philippians 1:27). Then, in Colossians 2:2 Paul says he wants everyone to have the spiritual wealth that comes from "the full assurance of understanding, resulting in a true knowledge of God's mystery." The phrase "full assurance of understanding" is a literal translation of *tēs plērophorias tēs suneseōs*, and it affirms exactly what I am talking about here.

Paul has more to say about such assurance in Colossians. In 2:7 he says the Christian's life should be like this, namely, "having been firmly rooted and now being built up in Him and established in your faith." Here the language of certainty is emphasized: we should be "firmly rooted" in Christ, which is the Greek word *rizoō*, meaning "firmly fixed on a firm foundation." Also, regarding what we believe ("your faith"), we should be "established," or *bebaioō* in Greek, meaning "to make firm, to strengthen, to confirm."

In the same letter (Colossians 4:12) Paul states his desire "that you may stand perfect and fully assured in all the will of God." Here the word translated "perfect" in the NASB is *teleios*, which also has the meaning of "mature" and is so translated in the NIV. We may recall that an article cited above says that "maturity" is knowing you may be *wrong* about something. Here Paul says that maturity goes with being *fully assured* about what God says.

In 2 Thessalonians 2:15 Paul urges Christians to "stand firm" — to be steadfast, to take a firm stand; and also to "hold to" — hold on to, hold fast to — everything he had taught them, "whether by word of mouth or by letter from us." Paul uses the verb "stand firm" (*stēkō*) several other times, urging Christians to take a firm stand on what they believe (see

1 Corinthians 16:13; Gal. 5:1; Philippians 1:27; 4:1; 1 Thessalonians 3:8). The word for "hold to" (in 2 Thessalonians 2:15 — *krateō*) is often used for holding fast to something so that it will not be lost or taken away (e.g., Hebrews 4:14; 6:18; Rev. 2:25; 3:11). A similar word (*antechō*) is used in Titus 1:9 when Paul says that an elder must be "holding fast the faithful word which is in accord with the teaching," so he can exhort in sound doctrine and refute those who contradict it.

In 2 Timothy 3:14 Paul exhorts Timothy, "Continue in the things you have learned and become convinced of, knowing from whom you learned them." This teaches us to "become convinced of" the things we have learned.

To this we will add one more text, from Hebrews 10:22-23, which exhorts us thus: "Let us draw near with a sincere heart in full assurance of faith…. Let us hold fast the confession of our hope without wavering" ("unswervingly," NIV). Here we will notice a threefold description of the sense of certainty we are to cultivate about what we believe: "full assurance of faith"; "hold fast the confession"; "without wavering." No wonder the same author affirms (Hebrews 11:1) that "faith is the assurance of things hoped for," and "the conviction of things not seen." Here "assurance" is the Greek *hupostasis*, "confidence, conviction" (see 2 Corinthians 9:4; 11:17; Hebrews 3:14), and "conviction" is *elengchos*, "proof, inner conviction."

In addition to the above texts that teach us we must have a strong sense of assurance in our belief and understanding of Christian truth, I will add a few texts that show us how this spirit of conviction must be present when we are teaching and preaching this truth. Paul tells us several times that we must teach and preach *boldly* and *confidently*. In Ephesians 6:19-20 he asks for prayer about himself, that he may "make known with boldness [confidence] the mystery of the gospel, and may "speak boldly" as he ought to speak. In 1 Thessalonians 1:5 Paul says he preached to the Thessalonians "with full conviction." In Titus 2:15, regarding the things he is writing, he tells Titus, "These things speak and exhort and reprove with all authority." In Titus 3:8, regarding these teachings, he says, "I want you to speak confidently."

When we look back over all of the above texts, we certainly (!) do not see the Biblical writers telling us to be doubtful, cautious, skeptical, hesitant, unsure, undecided, or uncertain about what we believe and preach. It is in fact emphatically the opposite! Here is a listing of what these texts say about the attitude of *certainty* we are to cultivate and seek regarding how we understand "the faith":

1. *Hold firmly* to your beliefs (1 Corinthians 11:2).
2. *Stand firm* regarding the faith (Philp. 1:27).
3. *Have assurance* of understanding (Colossians 2:2).
4. *Be firmly fixed and established* in the faith (Colossians 2:7).
5. *Be fully assured* in all of God's will (Colossians 4:12).
6. *Stand firm* on your doctrine (2 Thessalonians 2:15).
7. *Hold on* to your doctrine (2 Thessalonians 2:15).
8. *Hold fast* to the faithful Word (Titus 1:9).
9. *Be convinced of* your doctrine (2 Timothy 3:14).
10. *Have full assurance of* your faith (Hebrews 10:22).
11. *Hold fast* to your confession (Hebrews 10:23).
12. Have faith with *assurance and conviction* (Hebrews 11:1).
13. Speak the Word with *boldness* (Ephesians 6:19-20).
14. Speak the Word with *full conviction* (1 Thessalonians 1:5).
15. Speak the Word with *all authority* (Titus 2:15).
16. Speak the Word *confidently* (Titus 3:8).

We must conclude from all of the above that the Word of God has one right meaning which we can and should discern, understand, believe, and teach — with full assurance, conviction, confidence, and boldness. I truly feel sorry for those who do not know *with confidence* what the one right meaning of the Word of God is. I feel sorry for preachers and teachers and elders who are suffering from this "peril of uncertainty."

THESIS NINE

If all the above are true, then we must conclude that it is God's preceptive will that all Christians have a UNITY of belief and truth — that we all hold to the SAME UNDERSTANDING of the one true and right meaning of all Biblical teaching.

This final thesis is the logical conclusion from all the rest. If there is indeed just one right meaning for all Biblical teaching, and if all Christians are expected and commanded to discern, understand, and hold fast to that one right meaning, then it must be the case that God is commanding us to have *the same understanding* of Biblical truth. I.e., it is God's preceptive will (his command) that all Christians have a UNITY of belief and truth, that we all hold to the same understanding of the one true and right meaning of all Biblical teaching. This is the UNITY OF TRUTH of which I spoke in the introduction. And if we are morally obligated to understand the Bible in the same way, failing to achieve this unity is a sin.

Many if not most of us will immediately resist and even condemn this conclusion as extreme, outrageous, radical, horrifying, divisive, or at least impossible. An article on "restoring unity" in the Restoration Movement (from *Christian Standard*, July 2017) says such an idea confuses unity with *uniformity*, and advises us to just live in tension between unity and truth. In his book *Union in Truth* (Standard Publishing 1994, pp. 90-91), Dr. James North says Thomas Campbell warned us not to confuse "what Scripture says" with "what you think it means." For example, at the Last Supper Jesus said, "This is my blood." Yes, says North — "That's what He said. What does it mean?" Then North explains that we can agree that Jesus SAID this; but the MEANING of what he said is an inference, or deduction, or a *conclusion* from what he said — and we don't have to agree on this.

I don't know if this is the right understanding of what Thomas Campbell was saying, but it is widely accepted as the valid way to interpret Scripture. And I regret having to say this, but I must: *I totally disagree with this approach to Scripture! Why? Because we cannot separate a statement from its meaning — its ORM, its one right meaning!*

I emphatically reaffirm thesis number nine above: It is God's will that all Christians have a unity of belief, a unity of understanding of the one right meaning of Scripture. My two main reasons for this are as follows. ONE, it is the logical conclusion from the first eight theses. If we begin with the premise that the Bible is the Spirit-breathed Word of God, we must logically proceed through the various steps I have presented in the next seven theses; and the final logical conclusion is that we are morally obligated to have this unity of understanding. TWO, the Bible specifically commands us to have this unity, as the following texts show.

The main text commanding unity of truth is 1 Corinthians 1:10, which says (in the *New King James Version*): "Now I plead with you, brethren, by the name of our Lord Jesus Christ, that you all speak the same thing, and that there be no divisions among you, but that you be perfectly joined together in the same mind and in the same judgment." In this verse there are three parallel mandates:

1. "That you all speak the same thing" [Greek, *to auto*]. This is the literal translation. Some versions say, "That you all agree."

2. "That there be no divisions [Greek, *schism* — just like the English] among you." This word is used in John 7:43, where it refers to divisions regarding who Jesus was. Some said he was a prophet; some the Messiah. They were dividing over the right interpretation of Scripture (cf. vv. 40-42). Let there be no such divisions among you, says Paul.

3. "That you be perfectly joined together" [Greek, *katartizō*]. The NIV says, "perfectly united." It is important to note that the verb *katartizō* means "to restore something to its intended or proper condition" — as used for the mending of nets (Matthew 4:21). So its meaning here is this: "to be perfectly joined together as God originally intended you to be." And what is this God-intended condition of perfection? Two things are mentioned.

    a. Be perfectly joined together "in the SAME MIND." "Mind" is from the Greek *nous*, which refers to *how* we think, and *what* we think. Having the "same" mind refers to *uniformity* (not just unity) in how and what we think. Thus when we study the Word of God, we should all come to the SAME understanding of its meaning. The next point is basically synonymous with this.

    b. Be perfectly joined together "in the SAME JUDGMENT." The Greek word here is *gnōmē* (pronounced *KNOW-may*), *f*rom the same word family as *gnōsis*, "knowledge." It refers here to the same judgment about what *conclusions* we should reach when using our minds.

The repetition at the end here ("same mind, same judgment") just emphasizes our moral obligation to have *uniformity* of doctrine, *unity of truth*. We should be of the same mind and judgment concerning the ORM of Scripture.

The next text is 2 Corinthians 13:11, where Paul uses the verb *katartizō* (see above) to instruct the Corinthians to *restore your perfect state*, or to *be made complete* (NASB), or to *aim for perfection* (NIV). Then he adds some other instructions, including *to auto phroneite*, which is the one that establishes our thesis. The verb is *phroneō*, which means "to think, to set your mind on, to form a judgment." The object is *to auto*, which means "the same thing," as explained under 1 Corinthians 1:10 above. This is similar to what he said there, i.e., "Speak the same thing." Here he says, "Think the same thing," or as found in various translations, "Be of one mind" (NIV), "Agree with one another" (ESV), "Be likeminded" (NASB). This must include the idea that what we believe to be true doctrine should be the same for all.

We now turn to Ephesians 4:12-13 for the same teaching. In verse 11 Paul says the Lord has appointed some to be apostles, prophets, evangelists, and pastor-teachers for this purpose (vv. 12-13): "for the equipping of the saints for the work of service, to the building up of the body of Christ; until we all attain to the unity of the faith, and of the knowledge of the Son of God, to a mature man, to the measure of the stature which belongs to the fullness of Christ."

These leaders are supposed to "equip" the saints. The word "equip" is our old friend, the Greek verb *katartizō*. Contrary to the NASB and the ESV (and other versions), "equipping" is not the best translation. "To prepare" in the NIV is not much better. "For the *perfecting* of the saints" (KJV and others) is best. Verse 12 says that our Christian leaders must do what is necessary "to bring Christians to that completed state of perfection" so that they may be able to do two things: (1) do "the work of service," ministering to others; and (2) build up the body of Christ.

Verse 13 is the key verse for our purposes. It states the goal or end result of this whole process; it shows what we should be trying to attain. I.e., we should keep on doing the things stated in v. 12 "until we all attain to the UNITY of the faith, and of the knowledge of the Son of God, to a MATURE man" (v. 13). Thus we must be seeking two things:

1. UNITY. What kind of unity? Our intended unity is described in two ways. First, it is a unity of THE FAITH (note the definite article, "the"), i.e., what we believe to be true, as in Jude 3. This is not a unity of the act of believing, but of the content of our faith. Second, it is a unity of our KNOWLEDGE of the Son of God, or the gospel truth about Jesus our Redeemer.

2. MATURITY — "to a mature man." This maturity is measured by a comparison with no less than Jesus Christ.

It is significant that this unity and maturity are mentioned together here. Unity and maturity naturally go together; unity IS maturity! And this passage shows that the unity is uniformity in what we believe. Until we reach this unity, we are still "children" (v. 14). The word for "children" here is *nēpios*, which means young, under-aged children, even infants. The thought is similar to the point of Hebrews 5:11-6:3, where the same word (*nēpios*) is used for those who have not progressed beyond infancy in their study and understanding of Christian doctrine. Hebrews 6:1 urges us to "press on to maturity."

We look next at two related verses, Philippians 1:27 and 2:2. In the former Paul says to the Philippian Christians that he wants to "hear of you that you are standing firm in one spirit, with one mind striving together for the faith of the gospel." The words for spirit and mind are *pneuma* and *psuchē*, used as synonyms for the spiritual side of our nature, with special emphasis on the unity of our understanding of "the faith." This is reinforced by the latter text, where Paul exhorts us to make his "joy complete by being of the same mind, maintaining the same love, united in spirit, intent on one purpose." The reference to "being of the same mind" (*hina to auto phronēte*) echoes 2 Corinthians 13:11, literally, "that you may think the same thing." It also focuses the thought of Philippians 1:27 on the unity of the way we think, by repeating the same verb and saying we should have "one mind" (*to hen phronountes*). This is a more accurate translation than the NASB's "one purpose."

Another relevant pair of texts are 1 Timothy 1:3 and 6:3. In each of these verses Paul warns against anyone who is guilty of *heterodidaskaleō*, a compound verb meaning "to teach a different doctrine." (*Heteros* means "other, different"; *didaskaleō* means "to teach.") In 1:3 he tells Timothy to "instruct certain men not to teach strange doctrines." In 6:3ff. Paul says that "if anyone advocates a different doctrine and does not agree with sound words," there is something seriously wrong with his mind and heart. This is similar to 1 Timothy 6:20, where Paul warns against *antithesis* (the accusative plural of *antithesis*), which means the same in English. In Greek a *thesis* is a position one adopts and defends; an *antithesis* is an opposing or contradictory viewpoint. All of this assumes that there is *one true belief*. This is why Paul is adamant, that we must avoid "the opposing arguments of what is falsely called 'knowledge' — which some have professed and thus gone astray from the faith" (1 Timothy 6:20-21).

One last text will now be cited, 1 Peter 3:8, where the Apostle Peter says, "To sum up, all of you be harmonious," as the NASB translates it. The NIV is similar: "Live in harmony." The English Standard Version is more precise, though: "Finally, all of you, have unity of mind." This is addressed to all Christians, and all of us are exhorted to have this virtue: "unity of mind." This is the Greek word *homophrōn* (used only here in the NT), which literally means to be "of the same mind." "*Homo-*" means "the same," and "*-phrōn*" comes from *phroneō*, a Greek verb that has to do with thinking, with the mind. So the "harmony" which Peter commands us to possess includes a unity of our thinking, a unity of our understanding, a unity of our beliefs.

These texts — 1 Corinthians 1:10; 2 Corinthians 13:11; Ephesians 4:12-13; 1 Peter 3:8 — establish the validity of our final thesis, that it is God's preceptive will (i.e., command) that all Christians have a unity of belief or a unity of truth, in the sense that we all hold to the same understanding of the one true and right meaning of Biblical teaching.

PART THREE
HOW SHALL WE RESPOND TO THE BIBLICAL DATA THAT GIVE US THE MANDATE TO SEEK THE UNITY OF TRUTH?

What does all of this mean? Just how serious is this issue of the unity of truth? How much does it mean to us? How can we apply it to the way we live, as individuals before God and as the church before the world?

I will begin to answer such questions by pointing out a comparison or parallel between the *commandments* of the Bible and the *statements* (affirmations of truth) in the Bible. Regarding the Bible's commandments, we have always understood that God our Creator has placed us under a law code, and through the Bible He has revealed the commandments that we as His creatures must obey. We know that we are under moral obligation to understand and obey all the commandments that are applicable to all people in this New Covenant age. We realize how important it is to identify these commands, to understand them correctly, and to live by them.

We know also that we have not obeyed these law commands with the perfection that would keep us in fellowship with God. I.e., we have sinned and have fallen short of the glory of God. But God has made it possible for us to be restored to fellowship with Him, through the redemptive work of Jesus Christ. And as our Savior he has given us instructions on how to receive and maintain this salvation. These instructions are also in the form of commands; but they are *gospel* commands, obedience to which brings us into and keeps us in a saved relationship with God (see Romans 10:16;

2 Thessalonians 1:8). Our obedience to gospel commands (believe, repent, confess, be baptized) is the God-given condition for salvation.

It is important to understand that we are saved by obedience to the gospel commands, not by obedience to our law commands. We still have laws to obey, but we are not saved by obeying them. I.e., we are not under the law system as a way of salvation; we are under the grace system (Romans 6:14). We are not justified (forgiven) by "works of law" (Romans 3:28), namely, by how well we obey our law code. Even though we still sin and fall short of perfection, God's saving grace covers our sins (Romans 4:6-8). Our past and ongoing disobedience is under the blood of Christ, and our sins are not going to send us to hell.

But at this point it is also important to understand that we are still under full obligation to obey the hundreds of law commands that apply to us in this New Covenant age. Obedience to God's law is what it means to be holy as God is holy (1 Peter 1:16), and this is what the Christian life is all about. We are not under law as a way of salvation, but we ARE under law as a way of life. Thus we must give our full attention to continuing to OBEY GOD'S COMMANDMENTS! We want to obey, and to obey perfectly. This is the goal for which we are striving. It is called *sanctification.*

But commandments are not the only aspect of God's communication with us in the Spirit-breathed Bible. Another main aspect of it is the myriad of statements of fact, truth-claims, historical data, and doctrinal affirmations that are stated as *truth* and which we are expected and commanded to know, believe, and understand. The point that I am making here is that we have just as much responsibility to know, believe, and understand the STATEMENTS of Scripture as we have to know, understand, and obey the COMMANDS of Scripture. We take the commands of the Bible seriously; why should we take the Bible's revealed statements of fact any less seriously?

We know that God's Word is truth, and that this truth is spelled out in detail in the Bible, both in the Old Testament and in the New

Testament. Statements of truth are there, right alongside the law commands. And we also know, or should know, that just as we have disobeyed the commands, so also we have been guilty of wrong interpretations of many Biblical truth statements. We have been guilty of false teaching, and maybe still are in some of our beliefs. And we should know that believing and teaching false doctrine is *just as sinful as disobeying a command of God.*

Just as with God's commands, so also with the truth statements: some are essential for fellowship with God, and some are not. Just as there are gospel commands which must be obeyed for salvation, so are there gospel truths which must be believed and understood for salvation. For example, we must believe in God as revealed in Scripture (Hebrews 11:6); we must believe that Jesus is the redeeming Christ and the divine Son of God (John 20:31); and we must believe in His saving death and resurrection (Romans 3:25; 10:9-10). Likewise, just as most law commands can be disobeyed and the disobedience forgiven, so also can most of the Bible's truth-claims be disbelieved or falsely understood, and the false belief forgiven by the blood of Jesus. These sins of false belief will not send us to hell.

Yet, we remember that the law-breaking sins that are forgiven ARE STILL SINS, and with genuine repentance we want to get rid of those sins with all our hearts! Likewise, we must conclude that our forgiven false beliefs ARE STILL FALSE DOCTRINES, and with genuine repentance we should want to correct those false ideas with all our hearts! Just as perfect obedience is our only acceptable goal (Matthew 5:48; 1 Peter 1:16), so should perfect belief and perfect understanding of God's revealed truth be our only acceptable goal! Holiness of the truth as processed by the mind (Ephesians 4:24) is as much a part of sanctification as is holiness of outward obedience.

We are not saved by perfect doctrinal belief and understanding, any more than we are saved by perfect moral obedience to all the commands of God. But *both* are our God-commanded obligation and the God-intended goal of our Christian lives. How can we be any less serious about believing and understanding God's revealed truth than we are about serving and worshiping Him by obeying His revealed commands?

If we want to be serious about this, what can we do that is different from what we have already been doing? There is no doubt that we are under a divine mandate to seek, understand, and teach the one right meaning (ORM) of Scripture, and to grow into the unity of truth to the glory of God. What can we do to achieve this goal?

Here are a few suggestions. First, we need to *repent* (i.e., feel guilty about, feel sorry for, and repudiate) some very prevalent causes for our indifference toward sound doctrine, e.g., our tolerance of relativism and agnosticism, our pragmatism in the interests of worldly success, our laziness, our elevation of unity over truth, and our elevation of the love of man over the love of God.

Second, we must put more emphasis on *teaching Bible doctrine*, beginning with a restoration of the place of "Sunday school" in our church life and activities. This begins with serious planning as to the content of what is taught in the classes, namely, serious attention to Bible content. A regular curriculum should include studies of Bible history, Bible introduction, Bible exegesis, and Bible doctrine. Also, we should INSIST that all church members attend an appropriate class. (We will probably have to show them the Biblical mandate presented here concerning the learning and understanding of Scripture.)

To get this done we will have to fight and eliminate the "Peter Pan Syndrome" that affects so many churches today. Remember that Peter Pan wanted to be a child forever. His motto was, "I don't want to grow up." When I read Ephesians 4:11-16, I can see that this is exactly what Paul is talking about in our church life. We should be striving to reach maturity, he says (v. 13). Then we would "no longer be children, tossed here and there by waves and carried about by every wind of doctrine, by the trickery of men, by craftiness in deceitful scheming" (v. 14). We are supposed to "grow up" by speaking the truth in love, he says in verse 15! I fear we have too many Peter Pans in our pews — and in our pulpits.

To get serious about the unity of truth we will also have to fight and eliminate the "Pinocchio Syndrome." Remember that when Pinocchio told a lie, his nose got longer. What if a Christian's nose got longer for every false doctrine he or she believes is true? For you preachers, when you face your congregation from the pulpit on the Lord's Day, would you see a room full of people with long noses? This is actually happening in many of our churches [not the long nose part], especially the larger, faster-growing ones: doctrinal issues are kept in the background, and new members from all backgrounds are being welcomed and added into membership with little or no effort to correct their false denominational beliefs. Their Catholicism, Calvinism, Zwinglianism, Pentecostalism, feminism, annihilationism, pacifism, premillennialism, evolutionism, works salvation, original sin, infant baptism, "once saved, always saved," love-only God — these and other false doctrines lie dormant in their minds, unchallenged. Thus we can and do have large, active churches full of long-nosed Pinocchios, many of whom proceed to become teachers and elders who perpetuate their winds and waves of false doctrine (Ephesians 4:14).

Third, here are some suggestions for the preacher (senior minister, lead minister) of the local congregation, on how to take a larger role in teaching the Bible to your people. Start by taking on the task of teaching a Sunday school class in addition to preaching. This used to be standard procedure, but somehow it has become the exception rather than the rule. Who in most congregations is more qualified to teach thus than the senior minister? If this cannot work because of dual-service scheduling, then the senior minister should teach a regular, special, required class on Bible doctrine to all teachers and leaders. In fact, this should be done even if he is also teaching a Sunday school class. Also, make Bible content the top priority in sermons. Address current issues and personal needs by relating them to sound Bible doctrine and the Christian world view. Finally, get over the Satanic lie that we have no right to JUDGE what others believe and teach. It is true that we cannot judge motives of the heart, and cannot judge who will ultimately be in heaven or hell. But we can and absolutely must JUDGE DOCTRINE as true or false. Remember Titus 1:9, where Paul says that elders must be "holding fast the faithful word which is in accordance with the teaching, so that he will be able both to exhort in sound doctrine and to refute those who contradict." See Paul's further instruction to elders in Acts 20:28-31.

Fourth, I suggest that all staff members, whatever their professional specialty, should actually specialize in teaching sound doctrine. Administrative skills may be necessary and important, but they should always be subservient to teaching.

Finally, I believe we as a brotherhood need to restore the Bible College (or Bible Institute) model for the training of church leaders. For many reasons we seem to have evolved away from this, to the detriment of churches, church leaders, and individual Christians in general. We do still have some colleges that are keeping this focus, and these should be supported and encouraged; and potential ministers should seek them out.

CONCLUSION

In conclusion, we must understand that acquiring a correct understanding of the ORM — the one right meaning — of every Biblical statement or teaching is a life-long process that probably will not be achieved by anyone in this lifetime, any more than achieving perfect moral character will happen in this world. We all begin our Christian journey as immature novices, with a lot of blanks and wrong ideas and long Pinocchio-noses. Growing in the faith includes correcting false beliefs and adding new understandings. At any point along the way we will probably be nursing false beliefs, but we must always be open to revising our understanding.

We must take care, though, not to use this inevitably slow process as an excuse for doctrinal indifference or doctrinal passivism. We must fight against the "I don't care" syndrome. God's mandate is that we grow up in grace and knowledge, into the UNITY OF TRUTH.

CHRISTIAN TRUTH
FOR A
WORLD IN DECAY

CHRISTIAN TRUTH FOR A WORLD IN DECAY

INTRODUCTION

Sometimes we greet one another with this question: "How are things with you?"

"*Things*?" What kind of "things"? Usually we mean, "How's your health? How's your family? How's your job? What's new in your life?"

But what if we broadened the scope of the question, e.g., "In general, do you think *things* in the nation are headed in the right direction, or have they gotten off on the wrong track?" Here we would be asking you to give an opinion about "what's happening" regarding such things as the respect for human life, the respect for private property, the respect for law enforcement, the effectiveness of our schools, the honesty of our politicians, the moral standards portrayed on TV and in the movies, the respect for Christian beliefs and standards, racial relations, and the integrity of the family.

What would your answer be? Over a recent six-year period the people who do the "Gallup Polls" asked the question above ("In general, do you think things in the nation are headed in the right direction, or have they gotten off on the wrong track?") at least 20 times. In 18 of these polls, over 60% said, "Wrong track!" In the last five polls, "Wrong track!" was the answer nearly 70% of the time. "Right direction" was the answer an average of less than 25% of the time.

This leads us to ask, what's wrong with our country? Yes, it is a mess! But WHY are "things" so bad, and why are they getting worse and worse? Why is there so much violence, killing, stealing, lying, cheating, child abuse, spouse abuse, and no-limits, guilt-free sexual behavior? Why is our culture so committed to lawlessness and amorality? Why do so many people have no sense of right and wrong, and no conscience? Why these apparent philosophies of life? — "Do whatever you want, or whatever you can get away with!" "Might makes right!" "Anything goes!"

WHY? Why is this uncivilized, amoral, destructive *behavior* so openly approved and promoted by the media, the entertainment industry, our educational system, the cesspool of politics, and the "powers that be" in general? I suggest the following answer to the "WHY" question: *there is so much wrong BEHAVIOR, because there is so much wrong BELIEF.*

A basic rule of life is that *behavior follows belief.* Put another way, *ideas have consequences.* Actions are determined by what one believes to be true, whether it is actually true or not.

I believe that the source of our problem is wrong belief, and one wrong belief in particular. Our culture has more and more embraced a *monster lie,* one of the most destructive falsehoods the devil has ever concocted. When I wrote the first version of this essay, I gave it the title, "The Big Lie." For the last 150 years this "big lie" has been growing in acceptance; and in the last 50 years it has become dominant in our part of the world, and has produced the moral and civil chaos that is threatening to destroy us.

I.   THE BIG LIE

What is this false belief? It is the widespread conviction that *THERE IS NO SUCH THING AS ABSOLUTE TRUTH* — in other words, *relativism.* We have lost our sense of *truth.* You frequently hear someone say, "You can believe whatever you want, but what's 'true' for you is not 'true' for me." "That's just your truth, not mine." All truth-claims are relative, as expressed in this familiar poem by Abraham Edel (d. 2007):

> *It all depends on where you are;*
> *It all depends on who you are.*
> *It all depends on how you feel;*
> *It all depends on what you feel.*
> *It all depends on how you're raised;*
> *It all depends on what is praised.*
> *What's right today is wrong tomorrow;*
> *Joy in France, in England sorrow.*
> *It all depends on points of view: Australia, or Timbuctoo;*
> *In Rome do as the Romans do.*
> *If tastes just happen to agree,*
> *Then you have morality.*
> *But where there are conflicting trends,*
> *It all depends, it all depends.*

Such conscience-numbing relativism explains why people of all stripes can lie, steal, murder, destroy property, and do all sorts of evil *without feeling guilty*! If there is no absolute truth, then there is no absolute right or wrong! There are no laws; there are no rules. People are *ruthless* because they are *truthless*. Truthlessness begets lawlessness.

We have seen how, in recent times, many have objected to the posting of the ten commandments in public places or on public property, citing a conflict of the alleged principle of separation of church and state. I suggest that the underlying motivation for such objections is that our liberal, truthless society does not want to admit that there is such a thing as commandments or rules of any kind.

Another example of such relativism is the widespread presence of the philosophy of *postmodernism* in our academic world today. The fundamental teaching of postmodernism is that there is no such thing as absolute truth. This viewpoint can be found in some places within the

Restoration Movement. One may look, for example, at a book entitled *Christian Apologetics in the Postmodern World* (IVP, 1995), and find a chapter entitled "There's No Such Thing as Objective Truth, and It's A Good Thing, Too" (pp. 155-170), written by Philip Kenneson, a professor at Milligan College.

Here are a few statements from Kenneson's essay. "I don't believe in objective truth" (p. 156). Objective truth "is corrupting the church and its witness to the world" (p. 156). "Christians need not continue to answer 'the truth question,' and the sooner we see that we needn't, the sooner we can get on with the business of being Christians" (p. 161). "I realize there are plenty of Christians who think it makes good sense to say that the proposition 'Jesus Christ is Lord of the universe' is objectively true ....But succumbing to such a temptation is deadly for the church. There is no place to stand and judge this statement as true per se. There is no view from nowhere" (p. 167). This proposition [that Jesus Christ is Lord of the universe] "can never be objectively true, nor should we desire it to be" (p. 158).

For another example, several years ago I heard a New Testament professor from one of our largest Restoration Movement Bible Colleges defend postmodernism in a public lecture.

One may find examples of this denial of absolute truth in any age, but it has never been as dominant as it has become in the last century and a half. I suggest we may trace this modern movement to 1859, the year Darwin's *Origin of Species* was published. This began the determined erosion of belief in divine creation, the significance of which will be explained below. Within fifty years a large segment of Christendom known as Liberalism had succumbed to anti-supernaturalism and had given up almost every central Biblical truth. After another fifty years the denial of the absolute had become widespread in both secular and Christian circles.

When I was a seminary student in the mid-1960s, the main theological trends in the non-conservative Christian world were the

"Death of God" theology (e.g., Thomas Altizer, Paul van Buren); situation ethics, i.e., the "New Morality" (e.g., Joseph Fletcher), and "Secularization Theology" (e.g., Harvey Cox). Van Buren wrote a perceptive and influential essay called "The Dissolution of the Absolute," published in the journal *Religion in Life* (summer 1965). Van Buren's conclusions included these statements: "People no longer seem to operate on the assumption of the Absolute .... We have become relativists .... Relativism means that we appear to be coming more and more to a consensus that there is more than one way to look at any matter, and that what is said can be called true or false" only according to the circumstances.

From this point on, relativism has practically reigned as king. Views and systems that would never have been tolerated just decades earlier now flourish. In the late 1960s and early 1970s, several rivals to traditional Christianity arose: the gay liberation movement, occultism, the New Age Movement, secular Humanism. See, for example, *The Humanist Manifesto II*, published in 1973. Within evangelical Christianity itself, the idea of sound doctrine was challenged by the rise of feminism and by attacks on Biblical inerrancy.

My point is this: what we are seeing in our present culture is simply the fruit of the poison tree of relativism — the rejection of the idea of absolute truth.

II. IN DEFENSE OF TRUTH

What can Bible-believing Christians do about this, if anything? Most importantly, we must remain committed to the reality of TRUTH — absolute truth. This is what makes us different from most of the world, and it is why most of the world hates conservative Christianity: we believe in absolute truth and absolute rules.

How can we make sure that we, our families, and our churches remain committed to absolute truth? How can we influence others to agree with us, and come back to this firm foundation? Some may immediately say,

"We must simply continue to preach the gospel of Jesus Christ to the world. Jesus is the answer. Just focus on Jesus."

It is, of course, true that Jesus is the only answer to the problem of personal sin; he is the only source of salvation from that sin. Also, believing in Jesus as Lord and Savior can make anyone *want* to do what is right, and his gift of the Holy Spirit can give us the *ability* to do what is right. But this misses the main point. These are after-the-fact responses to sin. We are actually facing a much deeper problem, namely, how can we convince people *that there is such a thing as sin in the first place*? How can we lay the foundation for the whole system of right and wrong?

An important and necessary fact is this: the crucial issue of absolute truth, and absolute right-and-wrong, is a much larger issue than Jesus as such. The Christian faith is not just about sin and salvation; it is not just about what people think of as "religion." It is a total *world view*. If we compare reality to a large jig-saw puzzle enclosed in a box with a picture on it, we must see that there are a lot more pieces to the puzzle than Jesus. We must recognize that Jesus is just a part of that picture. He is set in a wider, much more comprehensive framework.

The question of absolute truth is whether there is one right way to put ALL the pieces of the puzzle together. The answer is yes; this is the fundamental claim of Christianity. So how can we go about putting the pieces together correctly? As with any jig-saw puzzle, we start with the edge pieces, especially the *corner pieces*. I am suggesting here that there are actually *four* such corner pieces to the puzzle of the Biblical world view, and in the rest of this essay I will set forth what they are. My contention is that it is important — yea, crucial — that the church not only accept these "corner pieces," but that we continue to teach them strongly and often, especially to our younger generations.

The problem is that the whole world around us has lost these fundamental beliefs, and that is why the world is in such a mess. Without these four corner pieces, there will be no idea of truth. So what follows are the foundation blocks upon which truth — and a decent society — must be built. These are the bedrock of a peaceful, just civilization. Without these, "anything goes."

III. THE FOUR FOUNDATIONAL FACTS THAT MAKE TRUTH POSSIBLE

In this section I will explain the four corner pieces of the "puzzle picture" that constitutes *the Christian world view*. These are the beginning point for the existence of absolute truth.

A. The Fact of the Existence of God

The first corner piece of the Christian world view is belief in the existence of God. Most people say they are committed to such belief. In a 2013 Harris poll, 74% of U.S. adults said they believe in God. In a 2016 Gallup poll, the number was 89%. There are serious qualifiers here, though. In the Harris poll, though 74% said they believe in God, only 54% said they are sure of it. In the Gallup poll, the question itself was ambiguous: "Do you believe in God or a universal spirit?" This "universal spirit" concept, though, can include views such as pantheism, and "the Force" of Star Wars legend. Thus we can be sure that many of those who answer "yes" to such a question will have a seriously deficient view of who God really is.

Why is this a problem? Because even if you believe in God, *how you think of God* will determine everything else you think. Over a hundred years ago, a prominent theologian, James Orr, said, "The doctrine of God …lies at the foundation of all right thinking in religion" (*Sidelights on Christian Doctrine*, 1909, p. 8). (I agree — but I would leave out the words "in religion." I.e., "The doctrine of God lies at the foundation of all right thinking *period*.") Orr continues, "As a man thinks about his God so will his theology be all through." (I will amend that: "As a man thinks about God, so will his *world view* be all through.") One more point from Orr: "In principle, every question of importance which arises in theology is already practically settled in the doctrine of God and His attributes." (One more amendment: leave out the words "in theology.")

The point is that the true God, who is the foundation of all truth, is not just any general concept of a "divine being," but must be the one and only God of the Bible. Believing in God is the starting point of the Christian world view ("In the beginning God . . ."), but it must be the true God, the God of the Bible. Unless one believes in God as revealed in the Bible, such faith won't make any significant difference in the way one lives and acts.

Exactly what is there about the God of the Bible that differs from most concepts of God, and which is foundational for the existence of truth? What is there about the true God that is so different that it can change the way we look at the world? Many will suggest that the answer to that question is this: God is LOVE! Therefore to know the one and only true God we must begin with Jesus and John 3:16. This sounds good, but it is not true. It IS true that the view that God is love is practically unique to the Biblical world view; but still, in our world view God's love is not the starting point, nor is Jesus the starting point of our world view. Rather, Jesus is the climax or conclusion of our world view. The Christian world view does not begin with Jesus; it ENDS with Jesus as the capstone.

Others will suggest that what makes the Biblical view of God foundational for the Biblical world view is the supremacy of His metaphysical nature, expressed in such attributes as his sovereignty (lordship) over all things, or his infinite power (omnipotence). Here we are getting closer to the aspect of God that makes Him exist and reign as the *true* God, contrary to the so-called gods of paganism. This unique understanding of God is not an attribute as such; rather, it has to do with *how God relates to the rest of existing reality*, including ourselves and the universe in which we live.

Here is a hint: it is crucial to understand that God is *not a part of the universe* — and thus is not finite and limited as the universe is. Anything, including every human being, that is a part of our space-time world is *limited* by its position in that world's space and time. This is the main reason why people today accept relativism and deny absolute truth; it is the basis for Kenneson's claim (above) that "there is no view from nowhere." So, if there is to be such a thing as absolute truth, *someone* has to exist *outside* this space-time universe and its inherent limitations. And who is this "someone"? *The God of the Bible; the God of the Biblical world view!*

What makes God unique is that He *transcends* this and any other space-time universe, and He is therefore not limited by it. His *transcendence* is His most fundamental attribute, and it is the reason why He also has the attribute of *infinity*. God is infinite or unlimited in every way. For our purposes here, what is most significant is that God is infinite in His *knowledge*. He has infinite knowledge; He is omniscient. He does not indeed have a view from "nowhere"; indeed, He has a view from EVERYWHERE! (We will come back to this soon.)

This takes us directly to the second corner piece of the Christian world view, which explains why God is different from anything else in his infinite nature.

B.   The Fact of Creation

Of all that we know about the God of the Bible, nothing is more important than the fact that he is the Creator of all things. "In the beginning God" — yes! But what is the very next word? "CREATED"! "In the beginning God CREATED!" (Genesis 1:1). Next to the very existence of God, this is the second most important truth; and it is crucial for establishing the reality of absolute truth.

This is why (as I have suggested above) we can identify 1859 as the time when a near-fatal wound was struck against the Christian world view. With the publication of Darwin's *Origin of Species*, the theory of evolution began to undermine the concept of creation. Over the next decades even Christians began to question the truth of Genesis 1-11, and with it Biblical creation and the truthfulness of the Bible as such.

In recent decades we have seen a renewed attempt to restore and defend belief in the Biblical testimony to creation, thanks to men such as Henry M. Morris (cf. the Institute for Creation Research) and Ken Ham (cf. Answers in Genesis, the Creation Museum, and the Ark Encounter). In many ways we can be very thankful for this renewed emphasis on "creationism." However, I believe that in some ways the creationist movement has actually *weakened* the case for creation in the eyes of our general population.

Why has this been the case? Because the "creationist" folks that are in the headlines usually argue vehemently for "young earth" creation: the idea that creation as described in Genesis One happened only about 6,000 or so years ago, and thus that everything in the universe is only about 6,000 years old. Many Christians, for different reasons, believe the universe is much older than this, but what comes across to the public is the false idea that ALL who believe in creation are "young-earthers," and that Christians are saying that unless you believe in the young-earth view, you don't really believe in creation.

No matter who is right in this debate, it has left the impression that the only thing that is actually at stake regarding creation is *how long ago it happened.* However important this may be, this whole discussion has side-tracked us from the main point, which is the simple *fact* that in the beginning, whenever that was, GOD CREATED THE HEAVENS AND THE EARTH!

I cannot stress this point enough: everything about this universe, including the human race, owes its existence to that one original creation event when the eternal God brought all the matter of the universe into existence out of nothing — *ex nihilo!* This means that when we think of God, the first thing that should be in our minds is this: GOD IS OUR CREATOR!

I will indeed stress this point again: when we think of God, we should think of Him as our Creator; and when we think of creation, we should remember that it was *creation from nothing — ex nihilo.* The main point here is that God and God alone has existed forever, from eternity. He "alone possesses immortality" (1 Timothy 6:16). Everything else has a beginning. God did not bring heaven and earth into existence by "formation" — by re-working some eternal, pre-existing material He just happened to find lying around.

Now the question is, WHY is this so important? Because it all comes back to the question of the reality of TRUTH! You see, unless we have such a Creator God, *we have no absolute truth about anything*! Now we can see why our world, our culture, has lost its belief in absolute truth: *because it has capitulated to Darwin and abandoned its belief in the CREATOR GOD.*

Why is the reality of creation so crucial for the existence of absolute truth? Because absolute truth depends on universal, infinite knowledge (omniscience), and only the one who has created all reality has this kind of knowledge. One of the main arguments against absolute truth is that even the most brilliant human beings are *finite*; they are limited by their specific orientation in time and space and have an inescapably self-centered perspective from which to draw conclusions. This is called the "egocentric predicament." It is considered to be an unanswerable argument against absolute truth.

Such an argument can succeed, however, only if the existence and creatorship of God are ruled out. But the Creator God does exist! And the knowledge in the mind of the Creator God is *not limited* by anything; He has no "egocentric predicament" that makes Him ignorant of anything and requires Him to guess or speculate about anything. He and He alone has the "view from everywhere," as mentioned above. Thus we confidently affirm that absolute truth exists: it is the contents of the mind of God.

This includes ethical rules and norms. Since such norms come from the Creator God, they too are absolute. Because God is the infinite Creator, He not only has infinite knowledge of what moral choices are best for His human moral creatures; He also has the absolute, sovereign authority to make absolute rules and the absolute right to enforce them.

This is the right of ownership, which God has by virtue of the fact of creation.

I hesitate to say this, but I must. I believe that in many ways the church itself is somewhat responsible for the breakdown of our society because we have not stressed enough the fact and implications of creation. I have heard many Christians and Christian preachers affirm that our only business is preaching the gospel of Christ and personal salvation (the old "fundamentalist" gospel). Others have said that all we need to do is preach Jesus as our model for holy living and social justice (the old "liberal" heresy).

This kind of false teaching is still found in conservative Christian circles. Decades ago (April 19, 1981), an article appeared in the *Christian Standard* entitled "Making Jesus Central." It said, "If Christ is truly to be preached, then every doctrine and ordinance of the faith must be dependent on Him, His nature, character and deeds, for meaning.... It must not be on doctrine as *doctrine*, but Christ that we teach." This idea is so common that I have given it a name: the Christological fallacy. It is the idea that Jesus's main purpose is to be the one and only standard for *knowledge*. That is another way of saying that Jesus is both the center and the framework of our world view.

But I must point out again: the Christian world view is *bigger than Jesus*! It begins with these two fundamentals: the existence of the Creator God and the fact of *ex nihilo* Creation!

But even these are only the first two of the four corner pieces. What are the others? Here is number three.

C. The Word-Revelation of God's Knowledge to Us

The third corner piece of the Christian world view follows logically after the first two. We may agree that the content of the mind of the Creator God is absolute truth. But that in itself does not mean that we have *access* to that truth — that we can see into the mind of God — unless God decides to pass along some of that knowledge to us! But that is exactly what He has done: (1) The infinite God exists. (2) He is the *ex nihilo* Creator of all things and has absolute knowledge of all truth. (3) And He has revealed some of this truth to human beings in the words of the Bible.

This means that when we think of God, we must think of Him not only as the God of *creation*, but also as the God of *revelation*. The third verse of the Bible (Genesis 1:3) affirms this: "Then God **said**, 'Let there be light.'" One of the first things God did after creating the first man and woman was *speak* to them: "And God **said** to them, 'Be fruitful and multiply, and fill the earth, and subdue it'" (Genesis 1:28). Hebrews 1:1-2 can be summed up in the key words, "*God has spoken*"! He has used the words of human language to communicate with us. This is what we find when we read and study the Bible: *the very words of God*. This is how Paul describes the Old Testament Scriptures in Romans 3:2, *ta logia tou theou*, "the oracles of God, the spoken words of God." This is why we can believe in absolute truth: the omniscient God has spoken to us!

It is difficult for us to fathom what a marvelous thing this is: the almighty Creator of the universe has spoken to human beings in *human language*, in human words! This is something that Satan's minions (worldly philosophers and liberal theologians) have been attacking for at least a hundred years. A main theme of the liberal theology of the mid-twentieth century and afterward is a denial of *word revelation*. Many have taught that God has revealed himself in certain *actions* within this world, but not in *words*. Somehow, communicating in words is considered to be beneath Him. And language itself is considered to be too frail, fragile, and ambiguous to communicate anything accurately — especially divine things, even by God! (This is a major theme of postmodern philosophy, where words and language have no objective connection with reality. The speaker/writer can mean one thing by them, but the hearer/reader can never discern that original meaning and thus must read his own meaning into them.)

To such ideas I will reply by using one of Paul's favorite Greek expressions (e.g., Romans 6:2): "*Mē genoito*! Absolutely not! God forbid!

May it never be! By no means! ON THE CONTRARY!" The very fact that *God has spoken* shows that we *can* trust the validity of human language, language itself being one of the gifts of the Creator. This is seen throughout Genesis One ("And God said . . ."). It is seen throughout the prophetic Word: "Hear, O heavens, and give ear, O earth, for the LORD has spoken .... Hear the word of the LORD" (Isaiah 1:2, 10, ESV). Speaking to us in human language, Jesus as God the Son testifies to the truthfulness of all Scripture (Matt. 5:17-18; John 10:35; John 17:17). Paul affirms it: "All Scripture is breathed out by God" (2 Timothy 3:16, ESV). See also 1 Corinthians 2:9-13. Because God has spoken, we accept the words of Scripture as communicating to us the absolute truth that originates from the mind of God.

Thus far we have explained three of the four corner pieces of the jig-saw puzzle that forms the Christian world view: the existence of God, the fact of creation, and word-revelation from God. But there is one more thing that is needed so that God's communication of truth can become meaningful to us.

D. Human Beings are Made in God's Image

One might think that the first three cornerstones or corner pieces explained above would be enough to establish the reality of absolute truth. But that is not the case; these are not enough in themselves. There are many who will say they accept these three ideas (existence of God, creation *ex nihilo*, word revelation), but they still reject the reality of absolute truth. Why? The hang-up, they say, is not on God's side of the communication process, but on the human side. For an illustration, think of communication via radio waves. This requires both a transmitter and a receiver. You can have the very best, highest quality transmitter; but the message will not be received properly unless the receiver is also adequate. Just so, according to some skeptics. God as the transmitter may be revealing absolute truth in His Word, but we finite, puny human beings are simply not capable of receiving it with any certainty of understanding. So we still cannot claim that we have absolute truth.

For example, as mentioned above, a major theme of this modern age is the inadequacy of human language. Based on this assumption, it is argued that there is no way anyone can know for sure what anyone else is talking about when speaking or writing in any human language. Some apply this assumption to the U.S. Constitution; others apply it to the Bible. In the latter case the consequence is that we no longer have an emphasis on sound doctrine in our churches. What they are saying is this: even if we accept that Scripture is God-breathed, the communication process breaks down when we finite creatures try to understand it. Nearly everything is thus treated as a "matter of opinion," and so it is concluded that there is no longer any one right way to interpret most Scripture. "That's just your interpretation" is the mantra.

Here is an illustration of this approach. William Baird, a Disciples of Christ New Testament scholar, in his commentary on the Corinthian letters (*The Corinthian Church*, Abingdon 1964, p. 57), says that people are always reciting "chapter and verse" in Scripture to prove that something is true. But remember, he says, "human interpretation is involved." And "the notion that one particular understanding is true" – is "folly."

Another way of stating this alleged communication problem is to claim that there is by nature an uncrossable gap between the infinite Creator-God and us finite, puny human beings. This view says that nothing we may try to express or understand about the infinite God can come close to His reality. He is just too far beyond us for us to assume that we can actually know anything about Him or about His thoughts. For example, a writer in the *Christian Standard* (Nov. 20, 1983) asserted that human beings are "so small, so dull," so ignorant. But that's OK, as long as we recognize it. We can even "speak in praise of ignorance." Remember, "we are saved by grace, not by knowledge." Thus, we are "free to be ignorant," and we are free to disagree with one another about what's true or false. We are "free to tolerate dissent," because we are always "speaking distorted words out of ... ignorance."

Here is where the appeal to Isaiah 55:8-9 usually enters the discussion: "For my thoughts are not your thoughts, neither are your ways my ways, declares the LORD. For as the heavens are higher than the earth, so are my ways higher than your ways and my thoughts than your thoughts" (ESV). So how can we talk about absolute truth, even with divine word-revelation? We cannot, says our postmodern world. We cannot hope to understand the transcendent meanings of God's words.

What shall we say to this? First, it is quite ironic to see how eloquently and abundantly postmodernists *use human language* to express their attacks on the adequacy of human language, all the while fully expecting their readers to understand what they are saying and to agree with them. Second, it is likewise ironic to see postmodern skeptics quote Scripture to prove that we cannot understand Scripture (as in the reference to Isaiah 55:8-9). The irony itself is overshadowed by the obvious *misinterpretation* of the Isaiah text, where verse 7 clearly shows that the contrast is not between man's puny, finite attempts to speak of divine, transcendent things, but between man's *wicked* ways and *unrighteous* thoughts in contrast with God's holy and pure ones — which we are commanded to embrace and imitate. See verse 7: "Let the wicked forsake his way and the unrighteous man his thoughts; and let him return to the LORD."

The main point, though, is this. The idea that our human minds and finite understanding are no match for the divine thought processes is shown to be false by the fact that we as human beings are uniquely created in the image and likeness of God (Genesis 1:26-27). This does not mean that we share God's infinite divinity, which is inherently impossible; but it does mean that God and human beings are able to communicate with one another. Our minds and our intellect are patterned after God's own intellectual life. Our logic, our reasoning, our analytical abilities, and our language itself are created to match God's own mental processes. (The obvious difference, of course, is that God's mental powers are infinite, while ours are quite finite.)

Being made in God's image means that when God speaks his truth to us as recorded in Scripture, three things must be understood. First, whatever God says to us must *mean something specific*. A statement from God cannot be open to just any interpretation we want to place upon it. Second, since God deliberately chooses to speak His word to us, He must *want* us to understand it, and to understand it in the same sense in which He gave it. See Isaiah 55:11, "So shall my word be that goes out from my mouth; it shall not return to me empty, but it shall accomplish that which I purpose, and shall succeed in the thing for which I sent it." Third, because we are made in God's image, we CAN understand it in the same sense in which He gave it.

The bottom line is that the denial of absolute truth is an insult against God. It is saying that God's plan to make creatures in His image, with whom He can communicate, has failed.

IV. PRACTICAL THOUGHTS AND APPLICATIONS

What follows here are some miscellaneous thoughts about truth, including some ways we can make the pursuit of truth more relevant for ourselves as individuals.

A.   Seven Biblical Truths About Truth

Here I will list what I believe are seven of the most important statements about truth that we find in the Bible. They summarize what has been presented above.

1.   Psalm 118:27 – "Yahweh is God."
2.   Genesis 1:1 – "In the beginning God created the heavens and the earth."
3.   Hebrews 1:1-2 – "God …has spoken."
4.   John 17:17 – "Your word is truth."
5.   2 Timothy 3:16 – "All Scripture is God-breathed."

6. John 10:35 – "Scripture cannot be broken."
7. Genesis 1:27 – "God created man in His own image."

These statements themselves are *absolute truth*, because they are either spoken directly by God (by Jesus as God in the flesh) or spoken indirectly by God's chosen spokespersons under the power of God the Holy Spirit. We accept these statements as true, and we understand what they mean, because our reasoning and thinking processes are patterned after God's own thought processes.

Can we be *absolutely* (100%) certain that they are true and that we understand them properly? No. We are finite beings and cannot have 100% certainty about any matters of fact or about any of our conclusions. This might make some folks nervous: what good is having absolute truth if we cannot be absolutely certain as to its truth and meaning? Also, some might think this is a kind of contradiction. How can we resolve such problems?

Here is the solution: we must be careful not to commit the fallacy of equating absolute *certainty* with absolute *truth*. These are not the same thing. We do not need 100% *certainty* in order to accept a given statement as true — even *absolutely* true. When we properly apply the rules of reasoning, evidence, and logic in the evaluation of any truth claim, we can usually reach a level of certainty that is *beyond reasonable doubt*. This is presumed in the Biblical mandate for apologetics, 1 Peter 3:15 – "But in your hearts regard Christ the Lord as holy, always being prepared to make a defense [*apologia*] to anyone who asks you for a reason for the hope that is in you." We should not think of this as *absolute* certainty, but *moral* certainty. Moral certainty is the idea that when the truth of a statement is beyond reasonable doubt, accepting it as true is a moral issue. I.e., it is a SIN *not* to accept it as true.

The bottom line is that we have *moral certainty* that these seven statements (along with countless others in the Bible) are *absolutely true*.

B. More Emphasis on the Fact of Creation

Given its importance in the Christian world view, we need to spend more time studying and teaching about the fact of creation. We can take a stand on either a young-earth or an old-earth view, but we must not get sidetracked on this aspect of the doctrine. Whichever view we take, the deepest and most fundamental truth is that "in the beginning God created the heavens and the earth."

We need to spend more time studying about and teaching about God in His role as Creator, in His work as Creator, and about His nature as Creator. This is even more fundamental or basic than God in His role and work as Redeemer!

This applies to our understanding of our own human nature, too, since we are a part of the creation. We should accept these facts about ourselves: (1) Every human being as the offspring of Adam has two basic identities: Creature, and Sinner. (2) Every Christian, though, has three basic identities: Creature, Sinner, and Saint. (3) For everyone, our most fundamental identity is as a *creature* of God our *Creator*. This is where we must begin in understanding ourselves (e.g., our dual nature of body and spirit, our creation in God's image, our freedom of the will).

Most of us stop learning much too early about this fundamental aspect of our Biblical world view. We must never assume that we and others in our family and church know all we need to know about the fact and implications of creation, and about the nature and works of God as our Creator.

C. More Emphasis on the Nature of the Bible

In a way similar to the above, we need to spend more time studying and teaching about the nature of the Bible. I am thinking of the fundamental truths of revelation, Biblical inspiration, inerrancy, and authority. (E.g., John 10:35; 2 Timothy 3:16-17; 2 Peter 1:19-21.)

We need to remember the connection between the Bible and the Church. We must never forget that the Church is built on the foundation of the Apostles and the Prophets (Ephesians 2:20). These prophets are the New Testament prophets (Ephesians 3:5); the Apostles and Prophets together were the ones inspired by the Holy Spirit to give new revelation (and inspired teaching) in the inaugural years of the Church. This is how the Church and Christians in general knew how to live and worship under the New Covenant. The inspired teaching of these Apostles and Prophets was given orally, but some was also written down and became our canonical New Testament. This is still the authoritative truth upon which we build and build up the Church today.

Another key passage about the Bible and the Church is 1 Timothy 3:15, which says that "the household of God, which is the church of the living God, is the "pillar and support of the truth." The second word here is translated variously as "support, foundation, bulwark." This completes the picture of Ephesians 2:20. In the Ephesians text Paul says that the truth is the foundation of the Church; in 1 Timothy he says that the Church is the foundation of truth. The latter idea is that the Church's job is to make sure it is showing forth this truth to the world.

Thinking of the Bible as the foundation on which the Church is built, I have given a lot of thought to the way doubters and unbelievers attack the Bible as a source of truth. In so doing they are claiming that there are "cracks in the foundation" of the Church. These would be false attacks and false claims about the Bible and Biblical truth, seeking to expose alleged weaknesses in the Bible. Very early in my teaching career I prepared a series of lessons refuting these alleged weaknesses in the Bible's claims to be the inspired and inerrant Word of God. I called the series "Six Cracks in the Foundation." It could be called "Six Lies about the Bible." They are as follows:

1.   "There is no such thing as truth."
2.   "There is no such thing as word revelation."
3.   "The Bible is inspired, but not inerrant."
4.   "Jesus is our authority, not the Bible."
5.   "There is no one right way to interpret the Bible."

6. "I know that's in the Bible, but ...."

D. The Truth Will Set You Free

In John 8:32 Jesus makes one of His most memorable statements about truth: "You shall know the truth, and the truth will set you free." What does this mean? I have given quite a bit of thought to how this works, and I will sum up my conclusions here.

1. Truths related to ultimate issues:

a. You shall know the truth about TRUTH, and it will set you free from RELATIVISM.

b. You shall know the truth about FAITH, and it will set you free from SUBJECTIVISM.

c. You shall know the truth about INSPIRATION, and it will set you free from DOUBTS ABOUT SCRIPTURE.

d. You shall know the truth about CREATION, and it will set you free from MEANINGLESSNESS.

2. Truths related to Christian living:

a. You shall know the truth about REPENTANCE, and it will set you free from THE LOVE OF SIN.

b. You shall know the truth about the HOLY SPIRIT, and it will set you free from the POWER OF SIN (e.g., physical addictions).

c. You shall know the truth about the WRATH OF GOD, and it will set you free from COMPLACENCY TOWARD SIN.

d. You shall know the truth about SATAN, and it will set you free from DOMINATION BY DEMONS.

e. You shall know the truth about GOD, and it will set you free from IDOLATRY.

f. You shall know the truth about SIN, and it will set you free from PRIDE.

g. You shall know the truth about GRACE, and it will set you free from LEGALISM.

h. You shall know the truth about LOVE, and it will set you free from SELFISHNESS.

i. You shall know the truth about HELL, and it will set you free from INDIFFERENCE TOWARD THE LOST.

j. You shall know the truth about the REVELATION OF GOD IN NATURE, and it will set you free from APATHY TOWARD MISSIONS.

3. Truths related to good mental health:

a. You shall know the truth about CREATION IN GOD'S IMAGE, and it will set you free from LOW SELF-ESTEEM.

b. You shall know the truth about FORGIVENESS, and it will set you free from GUILT FEELINGS, from SHAME, and from your PAST.

c. You shall know the truth about the CHURCH, and it will set you free from LONELINESS.

d. You shall know the truth about HEAVEN, and it will set you free from SELF-PITY.

e. You shall know the truth about GOD'S PROVIDENCE, and it will set you free from WORRY ABOUT TOMORROW.

f. You shall know the truth about the KINGDOM OF GOD, and it will set you free from PESSIMISM ABOUT THE FUTURE.

4. **Truths related to spiritual security.**

   a. You shall know the truth about BAPTISM, and it will set you free from FALSE ASSURANCE.

   b. You shall know the truth about JUSTIFICATION BY FAITH, and it will set you free from DOUBTS ABOUT YOUR SALVATION.

   c. You shall know the truth about the RESURRECTION OF CHRIST, and it will set you free from the FEAR OF DEATH.

   d. You shall know the truth about the CROSS OF CHRIST, and it will set you free from the FEAR OF JUDGMENT and the FEAR OF HELL.

CONCLUSION

My conclusion is this. When we as the church contemplate what we have to offer this fallen and corrupt world, we must indeed continue to preach the gospel of Jesus Christ as the only way of salvation from sin. But we must also proclaim the entire Biblical world view as a system of absolute truth, giving special attention to the four corner pieces of the puzzle: the existence of God, the fact of creation, the reality of word revelation, and the image of God. We cannot expect "things" to get better in this world until and unless more people return to the basic truths of the Christian world view.

SECTION THREE

"IN MATTERS OF FAITH, UNITY . . ."

"IN MATTERS OF FAITH, UNITY; IN MATTERS OF OPINION, LIBERTY"

INTRODUCTION

In this essay I am analyzing the first two statements of the venerable Restoration Movement [RM] slogan, **"In matters of faith, unity; in matters of opinion, liberty; in all things, love."** It is well known that this "peace saying" was coined by a German Lutheran writer named Peter Meiderlin (or Rupertus Meldenius) in a work produced about 1627, and that it has been adopted and used throughout the history of our movement. I am not here concerned with its origin and subsequent history, but only with the way it has been used in the RM in recent times. (For thoughts on its origin and early use, see Hans Rollmann, "In Essentials, Unity: The Pre-History of a Restoration Movement Slogan," *Restoration Quarterly* [1997, 39/3], available on several websites.)

I am not a fan of this slogan. Correctly interpreted and understood, it can be valid and useful. But its terms are so ambiguous that (in my opinion!) in recent times it has not been understood and used correctly. Let me summarize the problem.

First, the common understanding of "essentials" is *essential for salvation*. I.e., the only doctrines we need to agree on (seek "unity" on) are those which one must accept in order to be saved. This is usually a very short list, involving the person and work of Jesus and how to be saved.

Second, everything else — all other doctrines — are deemed to be "non-essentials," and all non-essentials are then equated with "opinions."

Third, since they are not essential for salvation, all opinions — all other doctrines — are regarded as *unimportant* in the sense that it does not make any practical difference what anyone believes about them. It is simply irrelevant what positions anyone takes on these issues. All interpretations and approaches must be respected.

The ultimate result of this way of using the slogan is clear: it has the devastating result of watering down and undermining the very concept of truth; in effect it destroys the Biblical concept of sound doctrine. Of course, this is already happening for many other reasons, but this slogan is being misused to justify this trend. Thanks in part to the way we are using this slogan, true Christianity — as represented by the RM — is being suffocated by doctrinal relativism.

My purpose here is to explain this in more detail, giving examples, and to suggest how we may use the slogan properly and to good advantage.

I.   THE SLOGAN MISUSED

The first problem, which is inherent in the slogan, is that it immediately divides all doctrines into just TWO categories: matters of faith, and matters of opinion. As we proceed, we will see why this is a problem.

The second problem is the ambiguity of the terminology applied to these two categories. The form of the slogan as it is most often quoted is "In matters of faith, unity; in matters of opinion, liberty." Sometimes, though, it is stated thus: "In essentials, unity; in non-essentials, liberty." A hybrid version is "In essentials, unity; in opinions, liberty." Is there a "correct" version? Which are the better terms? Does it matter which we use?

Here we will proceed to analyze each side of the slogan (each category) in order, beginning with "In matters of faith, unity." What are the problems regarding the terms in this unity category? First, we will consider the expression, "matters of faith."

The term "faith" is generally used in two senses: (1) Subjective faith (the *fides quae*, or "faith by which" one believes). This is the ACT of believing. (2) Objective faith (the *fides qua*, or "the faith which" is believed). This is the CONTENT of what we believe to be true. It is the doctrine to which our minds give assent. In the expression "matters of faith," the word "faith" is used in the latter sense. It refers to what we as Christians are called upon to believe.

To say there must be *unity* in such matters of faith indicates that these are teachings which *all* Christians *ought* to believe, in the sense of 1 Corinthians 1:10, "Now I exhort you, brethren, by the name of our Lord Jesus Christ, that you all agree and that there be no divisions among you, but that you be made complete in the same mind and in the same judgment." I.e., we have *a moral obligation* to have "the same mind" and "the same judgment" in matters of faith. This exhortation to unity implies that there is only one true belief, one true interpretation, for such matters of faith. This understanding of "matters of faith" is correct in itself and would not be a problem if it were not uncritically equated with the concept of "essentials," as the next point shows.

What about the term "essentials"? When the word "essentials" is used in the slogan, the first question we should ask is: "Essential *for what*?" Often, however, this question is never asked, and it is just *assumed* that it means "essential *for salvation*." Other terms are then introduced, which reinforce this narrow understanding. For example, the essentials (matters of faith) are regarded as *tests of faith*. I.e., those who do not believe them do not have true saving faith. Or to put it another way, they are also regarded as *tests of fellowship, or terms of communion*. I.e., those who do not accept these essentials are not part of the true church; they are not our brethren in Christ.

This approach also has implications for the meaning of the term "unity." It is proper to distinguish between the *spiritual* unity of all who are saved and thus who are thereby a part of the one body of Christ, and the *doctrinal* unity to which Paul exhorts Christians in passages such as 1 Corinthians 1:10; Philippians 2:2; and Ephesians 4:13-15. We may have the former without the latter, since in these texts it is Christians (who already have spiritual unity) who are being exhorted to seek the latter (doctrinal) unity.

However, when "matters of faith" and "essentials" are equated, and when "essentials" are interpreted to mean "essential for salvation," this distinction is lost. Those who have *spiritual* unity will already have *doctrinal* unity, since the latter applies only to things "essential for salvation" and will thus already be accepted by all the saved. Thus the imperative for Christians to seek further doctrinal unity on non-salvation issues is ignored.

We will now discuss the second part of the slogan, the *liberty* category. Here we see further ambiguity and more problems. We must remember that the very structure of the slogan implies that there are only two categories. The definition of the first category as "essential for *salvation*" implies that whatever is not necessary *for salvation* must be relegated to the second category ("non-essentials" or "opinions").

What is meant by the term "non-essentials"? The meaning here, of course, will depend on what meaning is assigned to "essentials" in the first part of the slogan. Since "essentials" is usually taken to mean "essential for salvation," then "non-essentials" will naturally mean *not essential for salvation.*

What leads to confusion here is that this category is also called "matters of opinion," or just "opinions." What is meant by "opinion"? In the formal sense, an opinion is an individual's judgment as to what he believes to be true or false about any given issue, even matters of fact. But connecting "opinion" with "liberty" suggests something quite different. It implies that an opinion is a matter about which there is no one correct view, and thus about which one is *free* (at liberty) to hold whatever view he chooses. I.e., freedom of opinion means that one is not *bound* by moral obligation, rules of evidence, or principles of hermeneutics to hold to any particular view. On the other side of the coin, it means that one should be free to hold to such an opinion without judgment or censure from anyone else. Thus a "matter of opinion" is an issue for which there is no one true belief, and no moral obligation to hold to any specific view.

This is why "matters of opinion" can easily be equated with "non-essentials," with the result that opinions are non-essential *for salvation*, since they are the opposite of essentials, which are interpreted to mean "essential for salvation." An even more serious result is that (in practice) a "matter of opinion" becomes non-essential, *period*. It is "just an opinion."

The conclusion is that what one believes about a "matter of opinion," about a non-essential, *really does not matter*. It is irrelevant. Is this not what "liberty" implies?

The bottom-line question now is: what has happened to the concept of *sound doctrine*? The answer is this: the assumption that there are only two categories of doctrine, plus the equating of "matters of opinion" with "non-essential for salvation," is a literal *disaster* for sound doctrine. The approach is this: if it is not a salvation issue, then you and everyone else are free to believe whatever you want to believe on that subject.

Here I will relate a few examples of this disaster. First, several decades ago I wrote an article for the *Christian Standard* defending the inerrancy of Scripture. In response, an M.Div. graduate from Fuller Theological Seminary (with a B.A. from a Lutheran college) strongly disagreed with me in a letter: "The strength...of our movement is that we believe that Jesus is the Christ, the Son of the living God. This is our only creed." *Everything* else is a deduction or opinion. "The *only* essential is that Jesus is the Christ, the Son of the living God. *Everything* else is up for grabs," including inerrancy. (By the way, he said he was "seeking a parish" among our churches in Ohio.)

Here is another example. In his presidential address for the 2003 North American Christian Convention, Bob Russell said this:

Another common denominator of those churches that are reaching the masses is that there is a **high value placed on harmony** as opposed to dividing over secondary doctrines.

We have this great slogan, "In essentials, unity; in opinions, liberty; and in all things, love." Isn't that what they practiced in the New Testament church? They allowed for differences of opinion about the observance of the Sabbath and eating meat sacrificed to idols.

Growing churches practice liberty in opinion because they place a high value on unity. I would challenge church leaders to list what you believe are essentials, what a person must believe to be saved. Then allow for liberty in the other areas. Don't take an official, dogmatic stand about such items as millennial views or eternal security.

Take another step and ask, "Can a person teach or serve as a leader in this church and disagree on the nonessentials?" People have visited our church and said, "I sat in the class of a teacher who believes 'Once saved always saved.'"

I respond, "Yes, I know that teacher and I disagree with him on that."

They'll ask, "Are you going to do anything about it?"

I answer, "I guess not, as long as he doesn't make it a test of fellowship. I may present my view again in a sermon in several months."

This is quoted from Bob Russell, "Imagine God's Glory Revealed in Your Church," *Christian Standard*, 9/21/03, p. 12. Note how, in the third paragraph, he equates "essentials" with "what a person must believe to be saved."

Here is another example. When I was teaching in graduate school one of my better students had the desire to become a church planter. In private correspondence he related the following encounter:

My wife and I recently attended a nationally-known assessment for would-be church planters.... During the weekend we met a couple of times with our primary evaluator. This man comes from a Christian Church background. His job was to discern our potential effectiveness as church planters. His chosen method was often to dialogue with us about areas that he perceived as potential weaknesses.

One of these areas turned out to be my theological views about women in church leadership. Based on passages such as 1 Timothy 2:11-13 and 1 Corinthians 11:3, I understand that women are not to teach male heads of households. Our evaluator asked me to defend my view, which I did.

After we discussed this issue at length we were both ready to move on. Still, with a smirk on his face, he asked me this question: "So if a woman is teaching a man, which one is going to hell?" I responded: "Neither one, it isn't a salvation issue." He looked back at me with disgust and said, "Well, if it isn't a salvation issue, why does it matter? I leave it up to the individual to decide, if it's not a salvation issue."

Ultimately, when my wife and I were receiving our final debriefing the evaluator said, "With that legalistic attitude ...you won't be successful in church planting [in our area]. You will probably be all right where you're going, but you can't plant a church in several parts of the country and be that narrow in your thinking. It won't work."

For a final example, in an article entitled "In Opinions, Liberty," Dr. James North discusses a 19th century RM figure named Aylette Raines and his view of universal salvation, and also Barton W. Stone and his denial of the substitutionary atonement and the classical doctrine of the Trinity. Brother North speaks of these views as opinions as opposed to matters of faith.

Some make a distinction between *statements* in Scripture, and *interpretations* of those statements. Some of these statements themselves may be essentials, but the interpretations of them must be regarded as opinions. I remember Professor George Mark Elliott telling about the time he was corresponding with a Disciples of Christ leader about this subject. The Disciples leader declared that the essential truth that unites us all is that "Jesus is Lord," and he affirmed that he personally did believe that Jesus is Lord. Professor Elliott wrote back and asked, "Exactly what do you mean by that confession?" The Disciples leader replied and bluntly said, "You have no right to ask me that question."

II. A CLOSER LOOK AT THE TERMS OF THE SLOGAN

Under this main heading I will explain how the terms in the slogan, "In matters of faith [essentials], unity; in matters of opinion [non-essentials], liberty," *ought* to be used.

A. Essentials

First, what should we mean by the term "essentials" (or "matters of faith")? My main point here is to challenge the common but mistaken idea that "essentials" means "essential for salvation." Why is this wrong? I will give two main reasons.

First, to say that *only* "salvation doctrines" are "matters of faith" or "essentials" is contrary to the very nature of the Bible. What IS the Bible anyway? We grant the human element in its origin, but the divine element is decisive. The traditional concepts of revelation and inspiration lead to the conclusion that the Bible is the WORD OF GOD. As the Bible describes itself: "God has spoken" (Hebrews 1:1-2). "All Scripture is God-breathed" (2 Timothy 3:16). Scripture is "the very words of God" (Romans 3:2). God's Word is TRUTH (John 17:17).

What is God attempting to do by giving us His very own words in the Biblical documents? He is attempting to *communicate* with us, to transfer ideas and concepts from His mind to ours. Here is a question we must seriously consider: In His attempt to communicate with human beings, has God *succeeded* or *failed*? To put it another way, when God speaks His Word to us, does He desire to communicate a specific message with a specific meaning? Does He desire that this message be understood? Can it be understood? To answer anything but YES! to these questions is to say that God has *failed* in his attempt to communicate with us. This, of course, is an unthinkable attack upon God Himself.

If we truly believe the Bible is the WORD OF GOD, then we must also believe the following: (1) That every statement in Scripture, and every communication therein of any kind, has *one correct meaning*, that God intends it to be understood in *one specific way* — no matter what the subject is, whether related to salvation or not. (2) That human beings made in God's image are ABLE to discern what this one correct understanding is, by applying the normal principles of language exegesis. (3) That we are morally bound and obligated to seek, believe, and teach this one true understanding of God's Word. This includes the idea that we are morally obligated to *agree* or be of the *same mind* on God's words to us.

On this matter of agreement or unity regarding what we believe, we must note that this is the Bible's own requirement. See, for example, what Paul writes in 1 Corinthians 1:10, "I exhort you …that you all agree [literally, that you all say the same thing], that you be united in the same mind [Greek, *nous*] and the same judgment or decision [Greek, *gnōmē*]." These Greek words, *nous* and *gnōmē*, cannot be differentiated here (Kittel, TDNT, 1:717). See also Philippians 2:2 – "Make my joy complete by being of the same mind [*phroneō*], maintaining the same love, united in spirit [*phroneō*], intent on one purpose." Here we are exhorted to "think the same thing," and to "think the one thing." "The fundamental demand of [this] Pauline exhortation is a uniform direction, a common mind, and unity of thought and will" (Kittel, TDNT, 9:233). Philippians 4:2 has the same exhortation.

Continuing with further Biblical teaching on such doctrinal unity, Ephesians 4:4 says there is just "one faith." This should probably be taken in the sense of the *fides qua*, or the body of doctrine which is believed. In Ephesians 4:13-15 "unity of the faith" and "unity of the knowledge of the Son of God" are the measure of maturity. Another relevant text is Titus 1:9, which says that an elder must be one who holds "fast the faithful word which is in accordance with the teaching, so that he will be able both to exhort in sound doctrine and to refute those who contradict."

Passages such as these do not mean that we must "fight and argue" with one another over Biblical teaching, but we must earnestly and graciously defend the faith (Jude 3). To simply "agree to disagree" is not the Biblical idea of unity of belief.

Thus we conclude that the idea that only "salvation issues" can be called "essential" is contrary to the very nature of the Bible as the inspired Word of God. Indeed, *every* teaching in the Bible is important for something, or is *essential* for something! Isaiah 55:11 says: "So will My word be which goes forth from My mouth; it will not return to Me empty, without accomplishing what I desire, and without succeeding in the matter for which I sent it." What makes a teaching *essential* is not whether it is necessary for salvation, but whether it is something about which GOD HAS SPOKEN.

Here is a second reason why it is wrong to say that only salvation doctrines are essential, namely, such an idea is contrary to the nature of *necessity* or *essentiality*. Regarding spiritual issues, there are two kinds of necessity. I want to explain this by drawing a parallel between *right action* and *right belief*.

First of all we shall consider right *actions*, i.e., acts of obedience to the commands of God. It is necessary or essential to obey EVERY command of God, but we need to recognize that God gives two types of commands: gospel commands, and law commands. Obedience to the former has the characteristic that some call the "necessity of *means*," while obedience to the latter has the "necessity of *precept*." Necessity of *means* is the term some apply to those acts of obedience that are necessary for receiving salvation. This is what Acts 6:7 calls "obedience to the faith," and what Paul calls "obedience to the gospel" (Romans 10:16 [ESV]; 2 Thessalonians 1:8). This is the obedience necessary for receiving the gift of salvation. Most would place faith and repentance under this kind of necessity; others of us would add confession and baptism. These acts of obedience are essential according to the necessity of *means*.

The necessity of *precept*, on the other hand, refers to all acts of obedience to God's law commands given to us creatures to show us how to live holy lives. If we were to collect and categorize all the commands and precepts in the Bible that govern our everyday lives in this Christian era, that would be our *law code*. Obedience to the commands of our law code is what Paul calls "works of law," which we do not perform in order to receive salvation but in order to please God. Thus such obedience does not have the necessity of means (for receiving salvation), but it does have the necessity of precept.

(The expressions used above — "necessity of means" and "necessity of precept" — are commonly accepted terms for a commonly accepted distinction. The terms did not originate with me. I would personally rather limit the term "means" to faith alone, while recognizing that repentance, confession, and baptism are necessary for salvation in other senses. But for our present purpose I will continue using the terms "necessity of means" and "necessity of precept" to represent the two kinds of obedience to God's commands, i.e., obedience to gospel commands and obedience to law commands.)

The point is that obedience to some of God's commands is necessary (essential) for receiving salvation, e.g., Acts 2:38; Acts 16:31. But what about all the other things God's Word commands us to do, e.g., Romans 12:9-21, 1 Corinthians 11:24-26, and Ephesians 4:25-32 (to cite just a few)? What about obedience to our everyday *law code*? If obedience to everyday law-commands is not necessary as a means of receiving (or even retaining) salvation, does this mean it is not necessary in any sense? If, strictly speaking, salvation is not directly dependent upon keeping these commandments, can we then say that it *doesn't matter* whether we obey them or not?

NO! We cannot exclude them from the category of necessity — as Paul clearly shows in Romans 6! They have another kind of necessity – the necessity of *precept*. A precept is a commandment given as a rule of conduct. What this means is that if God has commanded us to do something, no matter what it may be, then even if it is not essential for salvation we still have an absolute necessity to do it! We have an absolute moral obligation to obey every command of God, even if it is not necessary for salvation. To disobey a precept of God is still a sin, even if we do not lose our salvation thereby.

One of the implications of salvation by grace is that we are saved through faith in Jesus Christ even though our everyday obedience to our law code is not perfect. This is what Paul is teaching us in Romans 3:21 – 5:21. But we should *never* take this to imply that such everyday obedience is unimportant, irrelevant, or arbitrary! Such obedience is still *necessary*, with the necessity of precept. Paul is very clear about this in Romans 6. In other words, though we are under grace and our sins are forgiven, SIN IS STILL SIN, and RIGHTEOUSNESS IS STILL RIGHTEOUSNESS. Though sin does not keep us out of heaven (Romans 3:28), it is still wrong.

Imagine someone coming to Bob Russell and saying, "When I came to your church, my Sunday school teacher said it is OK for Christians to get an abortion, or to gamble, or to own a bar, or to get drunk once in a while." Do you think Bob would say, "Yes, I know that teacher and I disagree with him on these things. But he's a good teacher, and I'm not going to do anything about it as long as he does not make these things tests of fellowship"? I seriously doubt that he would take this approach.

I usually like to say it this way: We are saved BY grace, THROUGH faith, IN baptism, FOR good works. I.e., even though we are not saved *by* works, we are saved *for* works (Ephesians 2:8-10). We are absolutely obligated to pursue good works throughout our Christian life, even though these are not the means of our salvation.

My point is this: we must use the same approach to *right belief* as we use for *right action*. What is true of *obedience* is also true of *doctrine*. As we have seen, *some obedience* is necessary for salvation, but this does not make other obedience *unnecessary* or non-essential. *All* obedience is necessary, *just because God has commanded it!* In the exact same way, believing *some* doctrines IS necessary for salvation, but this does not make other doctrines or teachings of Scripture UNnecessary or NON-essential. Just as some obedience has the necessity of precept, so some belief has the necessity of *decree*. It is *necessary* to believe even the non-salvation content of Scripture, *just because God has said it!* We are saved by grace, through faith, in baptism, FOR SOUND DOCTRINE!

We may also say it this way: Just as there is a "law code" we are obligated to obey, so there is a "truth code" we are obligated to believe. God's will for us all is not only that we be saved, but that we "come to the knowledge of the truth" (1 Timothy 2:4). We are obligated to KNOW the truth (John 8:32), BELIEVE the truth (2 Thessalonians 2:12), and LOVE the truth (2 Thessalonians 2:10). Just as in Romans 6:1 Paul says, "Are we to continue in SIN so that grace may increase?", so we may also cry out, "Are we to continue in FALSEHOOD so that grace may increase?"

As in the case of works as such, the sinner certainly does not have to understand, much less believe, the entire body of truth and sound doctrine taught in Scripture in order to be saved. Certain core concepts are salvation issues, of course — especially the truth about Jesus and His works, and about how to receive salvation. But with most Biblical teaching, one can be lacking in understanding, or even be in error, and still be saved. Just as we are not "saved by works," so also we are not "saved by doctrine."

But here is the main point: just because certain doctrines are not essential for salvation or are not tests of fellowship, this does not mean they are arbitrary, or irrelevant, or unimportant, or "just your opinion." As we said above, we are not saved by *how well* we obey the *law code*; but we are still *obligated* to obey it. Sin is still sin, and righteousness is still righteousness. Likewise, we are not saved by doctrinal correctness, or by how well we understand and adhere to the truth code. BUT WE ARE STILL OBLIGATED TO SEEK THE TRUTH, AND KNOW THE TRUTH, AND BELIEVE THE TRUTH, AND LOVE THE TRUTH, AND TEACH THE TRUTH — the truth about every subject taught in the Word of God. Truth is still truth, and falsehood is still falsehood. That we are not SAVED by doctrinal correctness does not mean there is no such thing as doctrinal correctness.

How does this affect our attitude toward others? All (including ourselves) who have obeyed and are obeying *the gospel* are saved, even though they (including ourselves) are no doubt lacking in perfect obedience AND perfect belief. We are all brothers and sisters in Christ, as fellow-sinners saved by grace. But we cannot condone false beliefs any more than we can condone unrighteous behavior. Being saved "for good works" (Ephesians 2:10) includes being saved FOR SOUND DOCTRINE.

So how does this affect this part of our slogan, "In essentials, unity"? "Essentials" (or "matters of faith") include all doctrines that are necessary for salvation, or that have the "necessity of *means*." But "essentials" *also* include every other doctrine or teaching that is affirmed in the Word of God, because these teachings have the "necessity of *decree*" (as parallel with the necessity of *precept* for non-salvation obedience). We are just as much obligated to seek unity in these doctrines as in the salvation doctrines.

A question that will not be explored in this study is this: how do we identify the doctrines that are essential for salvation? My brief answer is that these involve the person and work of Christ, and how to receive salvation.

Another question that cannot be explored in detail is this: if all doctrines are essential, but not all are essential for salvation, what other kinds of necessity or essentiality are there? Here are some suggestions: some beliefs are necessary for spiritual maturity as Christians (though not for salvation itself); some beliefs are necessary for Christian joy and assurance; some beliefs are necessary for the integrity of the true visible church; and some beliefs are necessary to qualify one for teaching and/or leadership roles in the church. (For a bit more on this subject, see my book, *Faith's Fundamentals: Seven Essentials of Christian Belief* [Standard Publishing, 1995; now, Wipf and Stock], chapter 1, "Truth Itself Is Fundamental," esp. pp. 16-22.)

B. Opinions

We are now ready to turn to the term "opinions," and to ask what we *should* take this term to mean in our slogan, "In matters of opinion [opinions, non-essentials], liberty."

First, it is important to note that the word "opinion" has two distinctive meanings. It is my opinion (!) that we have not taken adequate account of this distinction in our use of this slogan. [Note: I am not aware of anyone else who uses the terminology I am using here, i.e., *formal* opinions and *material* opinions. But these terms seem appropriate to me.]

First, sometimes the word "opinion" is used in a FORMAL sense. A formal opinion would be ANY view/position/conclusion/-judgment/belief which *anyone* holds on any subject whatsoever. Whatever we believe, for whatever reason, we can say (in this formal sense), "It is my opinion that . . ." We are simply saying, "This is my judgment, my conclusion, on the matter." Whether it is true or false is not the point; it is simply "what I believe" on the subject.

I call this kind of opinion a *formal* opinion because the *content* of it is beside the point, and so also is *how* we actually came to hold such an opinion. Thus one may say, "In my opinion, Jesus Christ is the Son of God." This just means, "I have come to the conclusion that Jesus Christ is the Son of God." "It is my judgment that Jesus Christ is the Son of God." "I accept as true the idea that Jesus Christ is the Son of God." Someone else might say, "I do not believe in a Trinity, so I reject the idea that Jesus is the Son of God." "It is my opinion that Jesus is not the Son of God." To refer to such judgments as *formal* opinions is simply to acknowledge that the human mind processes information (correctly or incorrectly) and comes to certain conclusions (true or false) about anything and everything.

In this sense the word "opinion" applies to *everything* we accept as true, whether essential for salvation or non-essential for salvation. For example, a Jehovah's Witness says, "In my opinion, Jesus Christ is not God"; but a traditional believer says, "In my opinion, Jesus Christ is God." Or, the Free Grace advocate says, "In my opinion, repentance is not essential for salvation"; but a traditional believer says, "In my opinion, repentance is essential for salvation." Or, a feminist says, "In my opinion, a woman may be an elder or a preacher"; but a traditional believer says, "In my opinion, a woman may not be an elder or a preacher." Or, a dispensationalist says, "In my opinion, a secret rapture will precede Christ's return"; but an amillennialist says, "In my opinion, a secret rapture will not precede Christ's return." These are *all* opinions in this formal sense; but this is NOT how we should understand the word "opinion" in the slogan, since in this sense it applies even to one's views on "matters of faith" or beliefs essential for salvation.

Regarding opinions in this formal sense, everyone has the *physical* (or metaphysical) *freedom/liberty* to hold any such view he chooses, or to draw any conclusion he desires, about any subject. This is simply what it means to have free will. But in matters where God has spoken, no one has the *moral* freedom or liberty to hold to just any view he chooses. The only opinions we have the moral liberty to choose are matters on which God has *not spoken*. In such cases our views are opinions not only in this formal sense, but also in the *material* sense, as explained in the following point.

The second sense in which one may use the word "opinion" is what I call the MATERIAL sense. I call them *material* opinions because the word "opinion" here refers not to the *presence* of a certain view or position in someone's mind, but to the *content* of that position. A material opinion is a subjective judgment or conclusion about some material aspect of reality, but it is a judgment for which there is *no objective* way of determining whether it is true or false, right or wrong. In fact, these terms do not even apply to a material opinion. Such an opinion is a conclusion about reality based not on some factual evidence outside of us, but on some preference, some liking or disliking, *within ourselves.* Any statement for which there is adequate objective evidence as to its truth cannot properly be called an opinion in this material sense. Rather, it is simply a fact.

For example, someone may say, "In my opinion, Gold Star chili tastes better than Skyline chili." This is truly an opinion in the material sense, because it is a subjective judgment about some objective reality. It simply means that this person prefers the taste of Gold Star chili over Skyline chili. Another person might say, "In my opinion, Skyline chili tastes better than Gold Star chili." This is an equally valid opinion in this material sense.

But what if someone says, "In my opinion, there is no such thing as Skyline chili. The only kind of chili that exists is Gold Star chili." Now, someone may actually hold to this opinion in the formal sense, as discussed earlier; it may indeed be his actual conclusion about what exists in reality. But whether this conclusion can be called "just your opinion" in the material sense is an invalid use of the term. To say that there is no such thing as Skyline chili can NEVER be an opinion in the material sense. Here we are talking about objective matters of fact; and it is a matter of fact, not a (material) opinion that Skyline chili does indeed exist. Quite simply, the statement, "There is no such thing as Skyline chili" can never be "just your opinion" in this material sense; it can only be either true or false.

The late New York senator, Daniel Patrick Moynihan, once said, "Every man is entitled to his own opinions, but not to his own facts." I.e., where facts are concerned, nothing is a "matter of opinion" in this material sense.

As applied to spiritual realities, there are an untold number of beliefs that are opinions in the formal sense, but which can never be opinions in the material sense. They can only be true or false. Here are some examples:

- Human beings do not have significantly free will. (False)
- A secret rapture will precede Christ's second coming. (False)
- Women are not permitted to be elders in the church. (True)
- Baptism is the moment of time when God initially bestows His saving grace on sinners. (True)
- It is not possible for a true believer ever to lose his salvation. (False)
- The Lord's Supper should be celebrated every Lord's Day. (True)
- Human beings are the product of divine creation, not chance evolution. (True)

At the same time, there are an untold number of beliefs that are opinions in both the formal sense AND in the material sense. Here are some examples of these:

- Should congregations have church buildings?
- Should congregations always *vote* on elders? deacons? preachers?
- Should the Lord's Supper be before or after the sermon?
- May we baptize in an indoor, heated baptistery?
- Should meals ever be served inside a church building?
- Should any products ever be sold inside a church building?
- How many cups may be used to serve communion?
- May musical instruments be used to accompany congregational singing?

Regarding any issue about which one may hold a *material* opinion, one may argue that a particular view (i.e., opinion) is *better* or *worse* because of circumstances (i.e., a matter of expediency), but in the final analysis no one view is *the true view*. Here, opposite views may be equally valid. Here, it may be that "one opinion is as good as another." Any view on such an issue is not just "MY opinion" on the subject, but "AN opinion" regardless of who is holding it.

It should be clear by now that for our slogan to make any sense, the term "opinions" should not be used in the generic, *formal* sense, because in that sense *anything* that *any* person believes or affirms is an opinion. The only sense the term should have in our slogan is the material sense. Only in this sense can some things be opinions while others are not.

Now that we have explained the difference between the two kinds of opinion, we need to ask this question: What determines whether an issue is or is not a matter of (material) opinion? In the area of Christian faith and practice, the deciding factor is simply this: *has the Bible said anything about it — anything at all?*

A material opinion is a judgment or preference about something for which there is no objective basis. In the case of spiritual matters this means that *there is no Biblical pronouncement about it*. It is a person's view of something about which the Bible is *silent*. On the other hand, anything about which the Bible has *spoken* —

- no matter how significant or insignificant,
- no matter whether related to salvation or not,
- no matter whether given through revelation or inspired prophetic utterance,
- no matter whether affirmed few or many times,
- no matter whether taught specifically or by general principle,
- no matter whether stated in simple or perplexing terms,
- no matter how many people agree on it —

CANNOT be called "just an opinion." HOW CAN WE PRESUME TO REFER TO ANYTHING ON WHICH GOD HAS SPOKEN AS AN OPINION?

And yet, we see this happening quite frequently in our movement! We see this kind of reasoning:

- "Once saved, always saved"? Not a salvation issue, therefore an opinion.

- Women teaching men? Not a salvation issue, therefore just an opinion.

- Substitutionary atonement? Just an opinion.

- Universal salvation? Just an opinion.

- Hell as eternal punishment? Just an opinion.

- The Lord's Supper on Sunday, every Sunday? Just an opinion.

- Original sin? Just an opinion.

- Resurrection of the dead? Speaking in tongues? Unconditional predestination? Secret rapture? Church polity? Not salvation issues, therefore just matters of opinion.

NO! NO! NO! God's Word has spoken about all these and other such issues. There is one true understanding of them all! Conclusions concerning such doctrines are not (material) opinions; they are either true or false! We must stop using this slogan, "In matters of faith, unity; in matters of opinion, liberty," to justify tolerance of false doctrine and in many cases the absence of doctrine altogether — as if (for example) the difference between "once saved, always saved" and free-will salvation is no more important than the choice between a Ford and a Chevrolet.

The only proper use of the word "opinion" in the slogan is about matters of *material* opinion, regarding which each person does indeed have the (moral) liberty to come to his own conclusions.

CONCLUSION

The bottom line is that this slogan can be of use only under the following conditions (otherwise it is more harmful than helpful). First, it is necessary that "essentials' or "matters of faith" NOT be limited to "essential for salvation." These terms must be applied to everything taught in the Word of God. If the Bible says it, it is morally essential to believe it and to understand it properly — just because the Bible says it. If we still want to talk about beliefs that are essential for salvation (which is quite proper), then we must have *three* categories of beliefs, not just two. In addition to the category of (material) opinions, there are two categories of essentials: (1) "Salvation essentials," or "matters of saving faith," which must be accepted for an individual's salvation and therefore are a necessary basis for the *spiritual* unity of the church. (2) "Doctrinal essentials," for which we must constantly be seeking to attain *doctrinal* unity in the church, according to the mandate of passages such as 1 Corinthians 1:10. These are the Biblical teachings for which the correct view is essential for purposes other than salvation. We are under a moral obligation to seek and teach the truth about these issues whether salvation is at stake or not.

Both kinds of essentials are "matters of faith," in the sense that we are obligated to understand and believe them, but not all are "tests of faith" or "tests of fellowship." Within the body of Christ we have spiritual unity with all who have obeyed the gospel, even though there are serious disagreements among us on many Biblical teachings. Yet we are morally obligated, insofar as we are able, to seek UNITY of BELIEF on every issue about which God has spoken. We cannot simply relegate these disagreements to the category of opinion.

Second, this slogan can be of use only if we are using the word "opinions" in the sense of *material* opinions. These are matters about which God has not spoken, and therefore about which there is no divinely mandated doctrine. These are the only circumstances under which we have true liberty or freedom to determine our own preferred view.

If you have been paying careful attention to what I am saying here, you will see that this slogan, rightly understood and applied, basically means the very same thing as another slogan to which the Restoration Movement is committed: "Where the Bible speaks, we speak; where the Bible is silent, we are silent."

"HOLD ON!"
THE TYRANNY
OF CHANGE

"HOLD ON!" – THE TYRANNY OF CHANGE

INTRODUCTION

I don't watch many movies, but the ones I like are those where the good guys are clearly distinguished from the bad guys, AND where the good guys are *clearly winning*! I hate it when the bad guys are glorified and seem to have the upper hand, and the good guys are being beaten down.

The problem is that in real life, this latter scenario most often seems to be the case! In many ways, this seems to be true today. The good guys are on the defensive; the bad guys seem to be in charge.

Just so we are all on the same page, I will specifically say it: the good guys in our world are *we Christians*, and as Christians we seem to be the target of attacks from all sides. Obviously we do not like this, but we should not be surprised because of something Jesus said: "Blessed are you when others revile you and persecute you and utter all kinds of evil against you falsely on my account" (Matthew 5:11, ESV).

At the same time, in Romans 1:18ff. the Apostle Paul describes the pagan world itself as being filled with idolatry, lust, homosexual behavior, covetousness, maliciousness, murder, deceit, slander, disobedience to parents, ruthlessness, haughtiness, and all kinds of other evils. Then he says, "Though they know God's decree that those who practice such things deserve to die, they not only do them but give approval to those who practice them" (v. 32).

Here is the contrast: Christians are persecuted, while evil is celebrated! If there has ever been a day when these two texts are accurately describing the conflicts of the time, this is it. On the one hand, Christians are being reviled and persecuted for standing up for God's Word and God's way. All kinds of insults and ridicule are hurled against those who take a stand for faithfulness to Christ and to holy living. For example, just last year (December 2017) the Oregon Court of Appeals unanimously upheld a verdict that found a Christian couple who own a bakery guilty of discrimination against a gay couple for refusing to bake a wedding cake for their same-sex marriage. The Christian couple now must pay a fine of $135,000.

At the same time, evil practices are not only multiplying but are being glorified and praised and applauded by our liberal culture, just as described in Romans 1:32. Some of the biggest issues facing our country and our world today are a direct challenge to the values to which we hold as Bible-believing Christians. At the top of the list is abortion, which is constantly showcased by the public support of Planned Parenthood, for example. Close to that is feminism, which explicitly denies the Biblical distinction of gender roles. Controversies concerning sexuality keep getting more and more attention and support. This includes homosexualism as such, as well as same-sex marriage and transgender "heroics."

All of these anti-Biblical causes are heavily promoted in American politics, in the entertainment industry, in our educational system, and in most public media. One observer has remarked, "Try to find one positive portrayal of an evangelical Christian in a prime-time TV show now!" Hollywood (both movies and television) has portrayed the homosexual lifestyle as mainstream and normal, with continuing success. Here are some data from recent Gallup polls, which asked, "Do you approve of or oppose gay marriage?" In 1996 the response was, 27% approved; 68% opposed. In 2006 it was, 42% approved, 56% opposed. In 2015 it was, 60% approved, 37% opposed.

This growing anti-Christian trend is much more general than just a few ethical or social issues, as important as they are. For example, here is a report from the *AFA Journal* (April 2018, p. 9), from an item titled, "Study Finds Generation Z Least Religious in America." Generation Z is the name given to those born in 1999 and following, i.e., today's teenagers. (Generation Y, or the Millennial Generation, are those born generally in the 1980s and 1990s.) The report says that the Barna Group finds Generation Z to be "the least religious in the country's history, less likely to attend church services, and more likely to see science as superior to the Bible than older generations." By comparison, 13% of Generation Z claim to be atheists, which is about twice the percentage of adults in general (6%) and of the preceding Y generation (7%).

Over against this obvious trend toward secularism and relativism, those who hold on to traditional Biblical views of such things are attacked as the *bad guys*. The media usually make a point of glorifying and normalizing homosexualism, promiscuous sex, and now transgenderism, while depicting Christians as nerdy and creepy and idiotic and hopelessly behind the times. We are the *villains*!

This raises a serious question: WHY is there so much opposition to Jesus Christ and to Christianity and to religion in general today? Many of us are old enough to remember when it was not that way. So, why is there now such a gap between what the world thinks and what Christians believe? Why does the secular world look at the church as the villain? Why are we being reviled and persecuted and thought of as evil? Here I am going to suggest an answer to such questions, and I will try to explain what we must do about it.

I.   THE REASON FOR THE CONFLICT: THE TYRANNY OF CHANGE.

Modern western culture's most fundamental assumption can be summed up thus: *everything changes!* Indeed, everything MUST change. This is simply the nature of reality. Change is accepted as the unlimited, all-encompassing, all-dominating, all-controlling principle and force. Change is inevitable! Resist change at your own peril! In fact, change is not just good; change is *god*.

In early 2015 I was on a plane that had a little TV screen on the back of the seat in front of me. I was not paying close attention, but I noticed an advertisement that flashed quickly across the screen. I caught only part of it: "One nation under" — something. Being curious about it, I later did some internet research and found that what I had seen was an ad for a CNN series on the 1970s. The slogan for that TV series was "The Seventies: One Nation Under Change"! How appropriate, I thought: change has taken the place of God in our culture!

This mentality can be found everywhere, even in Christian contexts. Not long ago the lead trustee of one of our Christian universities was trying to explain to an assembly of students, faculty, and staff why so many drastic changes had been necessary in that school. I'll never forget the words he specifically uttered: "The only constant in life is change." Since then I have had private discussions with another leader of this same university who was likewise trying to explain the changes. Twice I was told, "Sure we are changing; but we have to, because the world is changing."

How did change become such a tyrant? My conviction is that it began with the acceptance of Darwinian evolution, with the publication of Darwin's *Origin of Species* (1859). Since that time the idea of evolution has been assumed to apply to *everything* — not just to biology, but to society in general. Everything is seen as evolving, as being "in process," as changing. That is just accepted as the natural way.

Traditional philosophies have argued about this. Some have declared that everything is always changing, notably Heraclitus (c. 535-475 B.C.). His deification of change is summed up in this quote from the Wikipedia article about him: "Heraclitus was famous for his insistence on ever-present change as being the fundamental essence of the universe, as stated in the famous saying, 'No man ever steps in the same river twice.'" Other philosophers have declared that nothing ever changes; all change, including motion itself, is an illusion (e.g., Parmenides, approximately the same dates as Heraclitus). Plato (c. 425-350 B.C.) tried to resolve the issue by creating the "Platonic dualism," i.e., there are two distinct realms of existence: the unchanging realm of being, and the constantly changing realm of becoming.

The philosophical debate continued until around the beginning of the twentieth century. From that point on, the major new philosophies created in the western world have been committed to the constancy and universality of change. Just before and after 1920, Alfred North Whitehead (1861-1947) was the major inventor of an entirely new philosophical system which was deliberately created to embrace evolutionary theory. It is appropriately called "process philosophy," and its metaphysics is all-inclusive: *everything* is constantly in the process of change, including God himself.

Other twentieth-century philosophies likewise have denied that there is any such thing as unchanging truth; relativism has been the agreed-on presumption. This applies to the philosophies of pragmatism, existentialism, linguistic analysis, and post-modernism. The last one, post-modernism, is the philosophy *du jour*; it is the current common excuse for ascribing change to everything.

The result of this kind of thinking is that *our culture has given up the very idea of truth*. In its place has come relativism, or the denial of universal, absolute truth. The mantra today is that each of us has his or her own "truth." And what is true for me as an individual *today*, may not be true for me tomorrow. We have seen this applied to the Bible, and in the same way applied to the Constitution of the U.S. Meaning is in the mind of the reader, not the writer. We have also seen it applied to common definitions, such as "human being," "person," "life," "marriage," "male," and "female." We constantly see it applied to "values" in general; what used to be considered wrong is now accepted as perfectly right and legitimate. This morass of relativism is often illustrated with this poem by Abraham Ebel:

It all depends on where you are;
    It all depends on who you are.
It all depends on how you feel;
    It all depends on what you feel.
It all depends on how you're raised;
    It all depends on what is praised.
What's right today is wrong tomorrow;
    Joy in France, in England sorrow.
It all depends on points of view: Australia, or Timbuctoo;
    In Rome do as the Romans do.
If tastes just happen to agree,
    Then you have morality.
But where there are conflicting trends,
    It all depends, it all depends.

Today we are bombarded with the "gospel" of change! In the social and political world the older term "liberal" has given way to "progressive" — a term which clearly embodies the idea of change. A recent president was elected in part on the appeal of his slogan, "Hope and change!" In April 1915 Hillary Clinton gave a notorious speech as the keynote speaker at a "Women in the World" Summit Conference. She discussed, among other things, how we can guarantee that "reproductive health care" — i.e., abortion — will be increasingly available to women. In answering this question she said [I listened to this video quote]: "Deep-seated cultural codes, religious beliefs, and structural biases have to be changed." As soon as she said this, there was immediate loud applause from the audience.

II. OUR RESPONSE TO THIS CHALLENGE.

How shall we respond to this kind of challenge? Here I plan to borrow a line from one of my favorite singers, Kenny Rogers. But that will come later. Right now, I want to give you some bad news and then some good news. The bad news comes first, and it is this: *many Christians, especially in our younger generation, have caved in to this seemingly irresistible tyranny of change!* They are joining in the chorus of accusation and criticism of the church. They are thinking that the church is "the bad guys" for resisting change.

I am not talking about any specific category of Christians. Actually my attention was recently drawn to this problem by a guest editorial in our local newspaper, the *Cincinnati Enquirer* (6/10/14). It was written by a young woman named Judy Hampel, a member of a local Catholic church. Her essay is titled "Time for Catholic Faithful To Speak Up" (p. A7). She laments the fact that "over the years, as the world has adopted a more inclusive and egalitarian attitude toward women, LGBTQs and other minorities, ... the church has lagged behind in incorporating these ideals.... I'm uncomfortable with church doctrine that excludes women from the priesthood and calls LGBTQ lifestyles sinful. These attitudes perpetuate misogynist and homophobic ideals that marginalize minorities and make all women and LBGTQs vulnerable to self-hatred and social marginalization on a global scale." So what should enlightened Catholics do? "Should we stay, and hope and wait for a new vision for our faith community, or should we leave in protest before we find ourselves counted among those who would perpetuate such a dark legacy for the sake of tradition?"

Judy continues, "It's time to make up for lost time. It's time for all Catholics and anyone else who will join us to collectively call to task all leaders and followers of any religion, sect or denomination that indulges in discriminatory doctrines and practices. Because, let's face it, one of the most compelling forces inhibiting universal justice is intolerance toward others, which is often perpetuated by religious archaisms.... We need to re-examine old doctrines and encourage a fuller truth and justice and mercy and unconditional love and acceptance and equality toward all. It's time to bring to fruition the hope that the religious scales will tip toward justice, mercy and tolerance."

Now (this is Jack speaking, not Judy) — I will call upon all Christians, especially the younger ones: *do not be lured into this whirlpool of deceit and destruction! Do not be shamed into yielding to the tyrant of change!*

I hope you do not get the wrong idea. I am not against change as such. Some change is inevitable, and some is definitely *needed.* Whoever is holding on to false ideas and doctrines and practices needs to change forthwith! This is the whole point of evangelism and repentance and conversion and sanctification. But here is where the good news appears, and here is where we can learn something from Kenny Rogers: "YOU GOT TO KNOW WHEN TO HOLD 'EM, KNOW WHEN TO FOLD 'EM!"

Here is the deal; here is the main point: *change* does not and cannot apply to everything! To try to make change into a universal principle — a very "god" — is anti-Christian and evil. At the very foundation of our Christian faith is this truth: *some things never change — they CANNOT change and WILL NOT change.*

The most basic reality that will never change is God himself. His nature, his character, and his purposes will never change. In Exodus 3:14, when Moses asked God to name Himself, God's answer was this: "I AM WHO I AM." God is the great "I AM." Speaking of Yahweh God, the psalmist David said, "Of old you laid the foundation of the earth, and the heavens are the work of your hands. They will perish, but you will remain; they will all wear out like a garment. You will change them like a robe, and they will pass away, but you are the same, and your years have no end" (Psalm 102:25-27). In Malachi 3:6 Yahweh declares, "For I Yahweh do not change." James 1:17 adds that with God "there is no variation or shadow due to change."

This likewise applies to God incarnate in the person of Jesus Christ. In Hebrews 1:10-12 the words of Psalm 102:25-27, cited in the previous paragraph, are applied to Jesus. Hebrews 13:8 adds, "Jesus Christ is the same yesterday and today and forever."

The same also applies to the spoken and written Word of God. Psalm 119:89 affirms, "Forever, O Yahweh, your word is firmly fixed in the heavens." In the same chapter, verse 160 says, "The sum of your word is truth, and every one of your righteous rules endures forever." In Matthew 24:35 Jesus says, "Heaven and earth will pass away, but my words will not pass away." Isaiah 40:8 declares, "The grass withers, the flower fades, but the word of our God will stand forever" (see also 1 Peter 1:23-25).

To say that God does not change, that Jesus does not change, and that God's Word does not change — together this means simply that the Christian Story does not change. All have sinned and come short of the glory of God; but Jesus is the Way, the Truth, and the Life for all who will surrender their lives to Him. This is the "eternal gospel" that we have the privilege of proclaiming to all who dwell on the earth (Revelation 14:6).

Here is where we have to "know when to hold 'em"! We have to know how to HOLD ON to the unchanging God, to our unchanging Lord Jesus, and to the unchanging Word given through the Holy Spirit! We cannot allow the pagan voices in this world to seduce us and intimidate us. They want to make us feel guilty for not being "modern," for not being "with it," up-to-date, on the cutting edge. They mock us and try to make us look foolish, old-fashioned, outdated, behind the times, antiquated, ignorant, politically incorrect.

Here is a warning: IT'S A TRICK! It's the DEVIL'S TRICK! See how Paul warns us in Ephesians 4:11-15: "And he gave the apostles, the prophets, the evangelists, the shepherds and teachers, to equip the saints for the work of ministry, for building up the body of Christ, until we all attain to the unity of the faith and of the knowledge of the Son of God, to mature manhood, to the measure of the stature of the fullness of Christ, so that we may no longer be children, tossed to and fro by the waves and carried about by every wind of doctrine, by human cunning, by craftiness in deceitful schemes. Rather, speaking the truth in love, we are to grow up in every way into him who is the head, into Christ."

We must constantly be on guard against the false ideas and sinful lifestyles being promoted by the pagan culture around us. They are like surging waves — tidal waves and raging floods of lies trying to sweep us away. They are like fierce winds of false doctrine that are trying to blow us around like tumbleweeds. Those who go along with these winds and waves are like weak, immature children.

So what does Paul tell us to do here in Ephesians 4:15? He tells us to do the one kind of change that we should accept and on which we should concentrate: "Grow up!" Become mature! Be strong and smart! It's the grown-ups that know when to take a firm stand on the truth, and to hold on to it. It's the immature, the infantile, the juvenile who allow themselves to be carried away by every new idea and every wind of false doctrine. You cannot stop these winds from blowing, but you can HOLD ON to the ROCK. So, HOLD ON to the truth of God's unchanging Word, while everyone else is being swept away by the floods of "change." Like Kenny says, "You got to know when to HOLD 'em"!

SECTION FIVE

THE PETER PAN SYNDROME

THE PETER PAN SYNDROME: CHURCHES AND CHRISTIANS WHO WON'T GROW UP

INTRODUCTION

In 1904, J. M. Barrie wrote a play: "Peter Pan, or the Boy Who Would Not Grow Up."

In 1983, Dan Kiley wrote a book: "The Peter Pan Syndrome: Men Who Have Never Grown Up."

In 2016, Jack Cottrell wrote a sermon: "The Peter Pan Syndrome: Churches and Christians That Won't Grow Up." (That's what you are reading at this moment!)

The Peter Pan Syndrome is defined thus: "A disorder in which a man is unable to grow into *maturity*," or where people "choose to hang on to their childhood in avoidance of assuming responsibility like a mature person."

My thesis here is this: Despite the widespread emphasis on "church growth," and despite the glorification of the concept of "megachurches," many churches (in terms of local congregations) and many Christians are suffering from this Peter Pan Syndrome. I.e., they need to GROW UP! And in many cases (if not most cases) it is the *church leaders*, including the *preacher*, who are responsible for this immaturity, because they themselves have not grown up.

This message is about *church growth* – the kind the Bible specifically talks about. When most people hear the expression "church growth," they immediately think of *numerical growth*, and *megachurches* — as measured by numbers. I am not saying there is anything wrong with congregations increasing in numbers; it's just that I don't see anything about numerical church growth in the New Testament, as some kind of goal we should be seeking. Maybe the New Testament just *assumes* that we will do all we can to see the church grow numerically. There is a Great Commission, after all!

But the New Testament *does* speak about church growth! The question, though, is – *what kind* of church growth? That's my subject here, as taken from Ephesians 4:11-16.

> [11]And he gave the apostles, the prophets, the evangelists, the shepherds and teachers, [12]to equip the saints for the work of ministry, for building up the body of Christ, [13]until we all attain to the unity of the faith and of the knowledge of the Son of God, to mature manhood, to the measure of the stature of the fullness of Christ, [14]so that we may no longer be children, tossed to and fro by the waves and carried about by every wind of doctrine, by human cunning, by craftiness in deceitful schemes. [15]Rather, speaking the truth in love, we are to grow up in every way into him who is the head, into Christ, [16]from whom the whole body, joined and held together by every joint with which it is equipped, when each part is working properly, makes the body grow so that it builds itself up in love. (English Standard Version, here and elsewhere unless noted)

This text makes three points. First –

I. THE CHURCH'S JOB DESCRIPTION
(vv. 11-12)

When we read verses 11-12, we find *the church's job description*. God gave the church a variety of church leaders, whose task is to equip all Christians to accomplish this purpose: "for building up the body of Christ." Body-building! We can think of this as Paul's term for "church growth," and he has assigned this job to every Christian. We are *mandated* to pursue church growth in this sense of body-building.

Who, specifically, is responsible for accomplishing this? There are actually two levels of responsibility. The *first* level (v. 11) includes several categories of church leaders established by the Lord himself: "And he gave ...." The previous context shows that "he" is referring to Jesus. The categories of leaders He has designated have the task of equipping all the rest of the saints (just a name for church members) "for the work of ministry," and that ministry is building up the body of Christ, which is itself the church.

Who are these Christ-appointed leaders? The first two categories, apostles and prophets, existed only in the first century of the church. They helped lay the foundation for the church with their oral and written teaching, which was inspired by the Holy Spirit and was the very Word of God. The very first priority of the church was to devote themselves to the apostles' teaching (Acts 2:42). When there were no longer enough apostles to teach in all the areas of the growing church, prophets were added to keep up with this task. In this way the church was "built on the foundation of the apostles and prophets" (Ephesians 2:20). These same servants have given us the blueprints for our ongoing building task, in the form of the writings of the New Testament.

The other leaders on this first level of body-building existed not only in the first century but continue to fill these roles through ongoing church history. Three are named, including *evangelists*. In a sense these are the *numbers* people, responsible for numerical growth. They preach the gospel and win converts, "bringing in the sheaves" and hewing out the building blocks from which the church is built — the "living stones" of 1 Peter 2:5. This is part of what we expect from the church's preachers or senior ministers.

Another group of leaders training others in body-building are the shepherds or pastors (these terms mean the same thing). This is another term for the *elders* of a local congregation, the ones who oversee the *spiritual* health and growth of the church. Another name for this group is overseers or bishops (these terms mean the same), indicating that these leaders have *authority* over a local congregation (Hebrews 13:17). Another main task of the shepherds is teaching (1 Timothy 3:2; 5:17; Titus 1:9). (Many preachers or senior ministers do a lot of this kind of work, and those who meet the qualifications in 1 Timothy 3 and Titus 1 could or should be selected by the congregation as one of their officially-recognized shepherds.)

The last group of equippers are the *teachers*. These are the workers who explain the meaning of the inspired teaching of the apostles and prophets, i.e., the Scriptures. The grammatical form of the Greek in verse 11 suggests the possibility that "shepherds" and "teachers" are the same category of leaders, with the implication that the shepherds (elders) and the teachers are the same group. These men would thus be "shepherds/teachers." In one way this would be appropriate, since a main task of the shepherds is teaching (as just noted). However, even if all elders are teachers, not all teachers are elders. Several times the spiritual gift of teaching is mentioned without any reference to eldership (Romans 12:7; 1 Corinthians 12:28-29). In both cases (elders who teach; leaders who just teach), though, this task of teaching the rest of the congregation is one of the most important aspects of the body-building work of the church, for reasons that will be seen shortly.

Of these five groups of leaders, the first two no longer are present in the church; but the last three are the key means of making sure the rest of the congregation is up to the task of "building up the body of Christ."

This leads me to mention that the rest of the congregation, the ones being trained at body-building, are the ones who have the *second* level of responsibility for accomplishing what Paul has outlined here in Ephesians 4:11-16. Their task is summed up in verse 12 as "the work of ministry, for the building up of the body of Christ." We should note here that everything that every saint (member) is doing as a part of the church is here called "ministry." The term is *diakonia*, which in this passage is a collective term for ministry or service of all kinds. "There are varieties of service [*diakonia*]," as Paul says in 1 Corinthians 12:5. In this sense we are all "ministers," or servants. The rest of this essay will show what God is expecting us to accomplish in our roles of service, as explained here by the Apostle Paul.

II. THE GOAL OF OUR BODY-BUILDING TASK
(vv. 13-14)

As with any kind of exercise or body-building regimen, we need to have our eyes on a *goal*. In physical exercise we might set a goal of achieving a certain weight, or a certain heart-rate, or a certain waist or biceps size. In like manner, here in Ephesians 4:13 Paul sets a goal for our spiritual body-building of the church, expressed ultimately in the phrase "mature manhood" (*andra teleion* in the Greek). The adjective is *teleios*, and is variously translated here as "perfect, complete, mature, full-grown." The content of the following verses makes it natural to translate it here as "mature" or "full-grown." In fact, in verse 15 Paul says specifically that we are to "grow up!" This is a direct rejection of the "Peter Pan syndrome" where Christians and churches are satisfied with perpetual spiritual childhood ("I don't want to grow up!").

In such a passage as this, where the Apostle Paul is telling us to be about the business of "building up the body of Christ," we should call attention to the sorts of things he does *not* specify as the object or goal of this task. First, he does not say anything about *numbers* — increasing the numerical size of the church. Given the Great Commission, we understand that this is always something we should be working on; but in this text the point is not quantity but quality. It is not how many bodies we can count, but the spiritual maturity of the *one body* of Christ, the Church.

Another thing that is not specified as the goal of our body-building efforts is increasing the *religious feelings* of individual Christians. The question we should be asking ourselves is not, "How can we make people feel good?" Though they may not realize it, many church leaders today seem to think that the real purpose of the church is to make people *feel good*, especially about themselves. And thus they emphasize *experience* in church services and church life.

This is, of course, typical of children, who have not grown up – playing, having fun, experiencing life, feeling good. In our experience-oriented culture this goal is often carried over into "adulthood" also. And for some reason some Christian leaders have made the assumption that it is necessary to carry this culture over into the church. We sense that postmodern seekers are coming to church, just daring us to make them **feel good!** Thus very often our congregational leaders will adjust themselves accordingly, and construct their public persona and assemblies around this dare: appealing to emotions, satisfying the desire to be entertained, providing the comfort of informality.

Worldwide, the fastest-growing denominations are all about feeling and experience. I recommend John MacArthur's fairly recent book, *Strange Fire* (a sequel to his excellent earlier book, *Charismatic Chaos*), which exposes this side of the Pentecostal and Charismatic movements. Referring to Aaron's golden calf, he says that many of the Pentecostals and Charismatics "have thrown their theology into the fires of human experience and worshipped the false spirit that came out — parading themselves before it with bizarre antics and unrestrained behavior" (xiv). They have elevated "the authority of experience over the authority of Scripture" (xvi). And they like to use the phrase "full gospel"!

Does this sort of thing demonstrate the church's maturity? *Really?* GROW UP! Your personal maturity is not measured by how excited you are, or how good you feel, or how much fervor and zeal are bubbling up inside you. This probably can and maybe should be present in our souls, but it must be the by-product and not the goal of our body-building task.

Another thing that is not mentioned as the goal of this task is *community service*. We are not told to measure maturity by the number of service activities for which we have volunteered and in which we have participated. In the last couple of decades a fad or trend has developed that is called "the missional church." The main idea is that we as Christians should do less "gathering together" in isolation from our community, and more "moving out" into the communities and cultures around us, engaging in service projects and social justice projects in the name of Jesus. There is nothing about this kind of activity here in our text, though.

I do not want to be misunderstood here. There is nothing wrong with seeking numerical growth, with experiencing feelings and emotions as Christians, and with living a life of serving and giving in our neighborhoods. Such things are needed. But what does our text SAY is the essence of maturity in the Church?

Here is the bottom line. In the text, maturity is measured in terms of *what we teach* and *what we believe* as a church. In other words, we grow up by feeding on truth and sound doctrine. Two things are specifically mentioned.

First, maturity will come when we attain *unity of the faith*. We are to keep up the body-building "until we all attain to the unity of the faith and of the knowledge of the Son of God." This is "mature manhood" (v. 13). Here the noun "faith" has the definite article: "*the* faith." This is not speaking of the subjective act of believing, but the objective body of teaching (doctrine) which we have accepted as truth. It is not just *that* we believe, but *what* we believe. It is "the faith that was once for all delivered to the saints."

We must note also that our maturity is measured not just by what we believe, but by achieving UNITY of what we believe, i.e., "the **unity** of the faith. We must all *believe the same things*. This includes especially and specifically a "unity … of the knowledge of the Son of God," i.e., what we believe about who Jesus is and what He has done for our salvation. It would be a mistake, though, to limit the scope of our doctrinal unity simply to Christology. This is a good place to start, but we cannot stop here. Our goal is "the unity of the faith" in general.

This requirement to have unity in what we believe is seen in several other texts. In 1 Corinthians 1:10 Paul appeals to us "that all of you agree with one another in what you say [literally, "that you all speak the same thing"] and that there be no divisions among you, but that you be perfectly united in mind and thought." He says almost the same thing in 2 Corinthians 13:11 when he exhorts us to "agree with one another" [literally, "think the same thing"], and he repeats this in Philippians 2:2. The Apostle Peter adds this in 1 Peter 3:8, "Finally, all of you, have unity of mind" [*homophrōn*].

Thus we must conclude that "mature manhood" comes about by pursuit of sound doctrine, and in particular, by achieving UNITY in our knowledge of true doctrine. *Until we have become UNIFIED in what we believe — in our understanding of Bible doctrine — we are still in a state of childhood — like Peter Pan.* We must take this requirement for *unity* of the faith seriously!

The second thing that Paul emphasizes here about achieving maturity through sound doctrine is that this maturity involves being able to distinguish *truth* from *falsehood*. In verse 14 he says that those who remain spiritual children are "tossed to and fro by the waves and carried about by every wind of doctrine, by human cunning, by craftiness in deceitful schemes." All of us Christians must be so trained in sound doctrine that we are able to identify false doctrines and defend the church from them. When our church members listen to radio preachers, and watch televangelists such as John Ankerberg, Reinhard Bonnke, Kenneth Copeland, Creflo Dollar, John Hagee, Benny Hinn, T. D. Jakes, David Jeremiah, Hal Lindsey, Joyce Meyer, Joel Osteen, Peter Popoff, Charles Stanley — do they know how to separate the wheat from the chaff, the truth from the false doctrine? If not, we are not building up the body of Christ!

This means that all of us who are leaders and teachers must know how to do this, and must specifically set forth an exposé of current popular false teachings. Also, we must teach and understand why we cannot accept the distinctive doctrines of groups such as Baptists or Presbyterians or Catholics or Methodists or Pentecostals. We cannot be hesitant or reluctant here! Many avoid this because they do not want to hurt anyone's feelings, or to seem judgmental. But here's the deal: if we are not doing these things, we are not building up the body of Christ!

We must have boldness to label false teachings for what they are: dangerous lies. It is not enough just to say, "Christians have different ideas about how to understand the wrath of God, or the millennium, or the rapture, or eternal hell, or baptism, or gender roles, or demons, or speaking in tongues. It is not up to us to say who is right and who is wrong. We are all serving the same God." NO! I can address such thinking only with Paul's words: "Grow up!" Get out of this Peter Pan mode of "doing church"!

For all of those who are evangelists and pastors and teachers, *it is your job to distinguish truth from falsehood*, to *expose* the falsehood, and to *teach* other Christians how to do the same! See Titus 1:9, which says an elder "must hold firm to the trustworthy word as taught, so that he may be able to give instruction in sound doctrine and also to rebuke those who contradict it."

And for the rest of you saints who are members of the Lord's Church, *it is your job to learn the sound doctrine taught by your leaders*. Do you really participate in Bible study activity, and Sunday school classes? If not, grow up! Get involved! Leave Peter Pan behind!

III. THE MEANS OF ACHIEVING THE GOAL
(vv. 15-16)

How is this goal of "mature manhood," as expressed in "the unity of the faith," to be achieved? What "exercises" can we perform in order to accomplish this body-building task? The good news is that these exercises are not physical in nature, such as push-ups and arm curls; they are instead spiritual exercises, accomplished with the spiritual activity of the mind and the heart. Paul sums it up in a phrase in verse 16, "speaking the truth in love." The basic lesson of this text is simply this: we achieve true spiritual growth by *what we do with "the truth."*

Paul says we must *"speak the truth."* In Greek this is actually just one word, a verb: *alētheuō*. (This is the verb form of the noun *alētheia, "truth."*) I suggest we use a new English word to translate this one Greek word, namely, TRUTHIFY. Just as we get the verb "beautify" from beauty, and the verb "glorify" from glory, so we can make up the word "truthify" from truth! So, if you preachers and teachers want to build up the body of Christ, you must TRUTHIFY – speak the truth, in love.

This means that we must acknowledge that there is such a thing as truth, which simply means *sound Biblical doctrine.* As Jesus says in John 17:17, "Thy Word is truth." This also means that we must preach more doctrinal sermons and teach sound doctrine in our Bible classes. "You shall know the truth" (John 8:32). Are we making sure this is happening? As the Church, we must teach and learn the truth about God and man and sin and salvation and the nature and work of Christ and the end times, for example. And while we are at it – we must expose the FALSE beliefs about all of these (see Titus 1:9). We must not only teach sound doctrinal truth as such, but also explain what it means and how to apply it.

And we cannot forget the other part of this duty: we must truthify *in love.* This includes love for God Himself as the source of this truth, and love for the truth itself (2 Thessalonians 2:10), and love for the hearers and believers of the truth, and finally a sincere love for the false teachers who are spreading false doctrines.

All of this presupposes not only the *existence* of truth, but also our ability to *identify* it (to distinguish it from false doctrines) and to *understand* it. I am extremely sad and impatient with the attitude that is so prevalent today, that the pursuit and preaching of sound doctrine is not only too difficult but also downright dangerous. (How often have you heard this demonic lie, "Doctrine divides; love unites"?) Do we want to grow to maturity, or not? Do we want to heed Ephesians 4, or not? Do we want to follow Peter Pan or the Apostle Paul? Many churches and individual Christians have seriously failed to follow Paul's teaching here. They are not growing into maturity in Christ; they are stuck in the Peter Pan syndrome! To them I say, "Grow up!"

What causes so many Christians to be stuck in the Peter Pan Syndrome? The answer: anything that denies or diminishes the essential role of SOUND DOCTRINE in the life of the church. My plan here is to name and explain five factors that widely exist in the Christian world and which undermine everything Paul is teaching here in Ephesians 4:11-16. These are all enemies of sound doctrine.

The first enemy of sound doctrine is the old philosophical demon, *relativism*. In general, this is the mindset that there is no such thing as truth, in the sense that nothing is always true for all people in the same way. The idea is that human beings are inherently unable to ultimately distinguish what is true from what is false, so "truth" simply does not exist. The modern version of this is called *postmodernism*.

As applied to the church, we can call it *doctrinal* relativism. This is the idea that there is no one true or correct meaning for any statement in the Bible. What the Bible authors themselves meant when they wrote the books of the Bible is impossible for us to know because of linguistic and cultural barriers; thus we necessarily must impose upon the Bible whatever meanings seem to fit best within our culture. We put the meaning into Scripture from OUR side (not from the authors' side). And it will not always be the same meaning – but that's OK!

As an illustration, we with our Bibles are like children with coloring books. But instead of adding to the pictures different colors of our choice, we are adding to Biblical texts different *meanings* of our choice. The result is that we have "every wind of doctrine" – but that's good!

What shall we say about this? Simply that relativism is the enemy of Christianity. You cannot be a consistent relativist and a consistent Christian. Why not? Because the Bible affirms the existence of truth. We **know** that truth exists from our very text (Ephesians 4:11-16), and from many others in Scripture. Scripture affirms the reality of truth, and the very NATURE of the Bible — as the *words of God* — requires us to believe that its words are truth. Jesus speaking to God the Father says, "Your word is truth" (John 17:17). Another reason we know there is such a thing as truth is that the very concept of *"unity* of the faith" presupposes that truth exists. We can have unity of what we believe ONLY if there is *one right meaning* of biblical statements. One more point is that the existence of *false* doctrine likewise presupposes that there must be true doctrine.

The doctrinal relativist may then say, "But every person has the *right* to believe whatever view he wants about such things as eternal security, the millennium, gender roles, baptism, hell, or whatever." No, that is not correct. We do have free will, which means we have the *ability* to accept whatever view we may want on any subject. But that does not mean that we have the *right* to do so. Where God has spoken, we have a moral obligation to believe it and to understand it as God intended it. This means we have the moral obligation to use our reasoning powers as installed within us by God. This is the *morality of truth*. We have just as much obligation to believe and understand the Bible's *truth* as we do to obey the Bible's *commands*.

Saying that truth is relative is one of the greatest signs of immaturity in the church. It is one of the most obvious expressions of the Peter Pan Syndrome. Ephesians 4:13 does not say that God wants us to achieve DIVERSITY of the faith, but UNITY of the faith. Also, consider verse 14 again: "so that we may no longer be children, tossed to and fro by the waves and carried about by every wind of doctrine, by human cunning, by craftiness in deceitful schemes." How can this be harmonized with the alleged relativity of truth?

I say to you relativist Peter Pans out there: GROW UP! *Truthify in love!*

The second enemy of sound doctrine is *agnosticism*. In actuality it is just a practical form of relativism and is just as destructive as relativism. Agnosticism does not deny that truth exists; it simply says that we finite creatures will never find it. In the church it becomes *doctrinal* agnosticism, or the idea that the Bible is true but we can never be sure what it really means about any given subject. For example, *who knows* what millennial view is the true one? *Who knows* what the cross of Jesus Christ was really about? *Who knows* what the real meaning of baptism is? We can grant that there is one right meaning to such Biblical teaching, but we simply cannot take a stand on what it is.

How does this agnosticism arise? Often it is based on a false understanding of the transcendent nature of God. OK, it is said – we agree that the Bible IS the *Word of GOD*. But *how can we expect to understand GOD?* He is so far above us; His ways are not our ways; His thoughts are not our thoughts. He is omniscient and infinite, and we are so finite and ignorant and puny. So how could we ever know what His Word really means? It is too mysterious and transcendent compared to our limited capacities. So says the agnostic.

How may we respond to this? Here's my thought: too often this is just an excuse for avoiding serious doctrinal study of the Bible. Is God omniscient? Yes indeed! Does this mean He knows everything? Yes indeed! Well, if God knows everything, doesn't that include the fact that He *knows how* to communicate with us on our level? Remember: God created us *in His image*, just for the purpose of being able to communicate with us. We are equipped by nature to receive His word and to understand it.

Jesus declares: "And you WILL know the truth" (John 8:32).

Hebrews 1:1-2 says, "Long ago, at many times and in many ways, **God spoke** to our fathers by the prophets, but in these last days **he has spoken** to us by his son." Has God spoken? Yes indeed! Has He spoken IN VAIN? No way!

To all you would-be Peter Pans who are doctrinal agnostics, I say: GROW UP! *Truthify* in love!

A third enemy of sound doctrine is *false humility*. This is something we must avoid if we are going to reach the goal of maturity. There are two parts to this false humility. The first is the common idea that it is somehow *arrogant* to claim to know the truth about anything. Thus to be humble we must never say, "This is what the Bible teaches!" We must never say, "This is the TRUTH about" a particular doctrine. We simply cannot be "dogmatic"!

This oh-so-pious attitude is seen in the famous quote from Gotthold Lessing (1729-1781), in *Eine Duplik* (1778), found in *Werke*, 8:32-33: "If God held all truth in his right hand and in his left everlasting striving after truth, so that I should always and everlastingly be mistaken, and said to me, 'choose,' with humility I would pick the left hand and say, 'Father, grant me that. Absolute truth is for thee alone.'" Modern versions of this are "Seeking truth is better than finding it" and "Believe those who seek truth, doubt those who have found it."

This kind of attitude sounds so pious — so, uh, *humble.* But here is my response to Lessing and others who share this attitude: What an idiot! If you can never have truth; if all your efforts to find it result only in mistakes and errors – why seek it at all? You've just wasted your time and done yourself harm as well. But this approach to truth is in fact a *false choice*, because in life we actually do both. We *do* have the truth about some things, while we are still seeking further truth about others. That is true in theology too.

Here is the other part to this false humility – it is the idea that we should never accuse anyone, especially by name, of being a false teacher. Who are we to judge someone else? They are just as sincere as we are, are they not? My response to all who believe this — and I say it in love — is this: you are absolutely wrong! God's Word **commands** us to identify false teaching and false teachers! If you think otherwise, YOU are a false teacher!

One main reason for seeking truth is to be able to identify falsehood. See Ephesians 4:14 again: "so that we may no longer be children, tossed to and fro by the waves and carried about by every wind of doctrine, by human cunning, by craftiness in deceitful schemes." Doctrinal agnosticism makes immature Christians "sitting ducks" for the destructive waves and winds of false doctrine. Let us take seriously Paul's instruction that an elder "must hold firm to the trustworthy word as taught, so that he may be able to give instruction in sound doctrine **and also to rebuke those who contradict it**" (Titus 1:9).

Such false humility is a form of the Peter Pan mentality. To such I say – GROW UP! Truthify in love!

The fourth enemy of sound doctrine in the church is something I will call *reductionism*. I call it this because there is a common idea in our Restoration Movement that only *some – a few* – doctrines are important enough to be concerned about. We should not worry about the rest; and certainly we should give everyone the freedom to believe whatever they want to believe about them. One way of doing this is to distinguish between (1) the doctrines or beliefs that are related to Christ and salvation, and (2) everything else. We will want to agree on the former, but can set aside everything else as unimportant.

Here is an example of this that I found recently by looking at the website of a local church here in Cincinnati, OH. In the "what we believe" section, this is said: "As far as we're concerned, the essentials are all about the identity and meaning of Jesus' life, death, and resurrection. In everything else there is room for dialogue, with each other, with our culture and with Scripture."

As is suggested by the reference to "essentials" in this statement, such reductionism often happens especially in connection with our Restoration Movement slogan, "In essentials (matters of faith), unity. In non-essentials (matters of opinion), liberty. In all things, love." At first this sounds good. But the problem comes when very little is put into the category of essentials, and everything else — most beliefs and doctrines — are put into the category of *opinions* — which are then written off as unimportant. Thus we wind up disagreeing about almost everything — but no one cares!

Here is an analogy: Think of the difference between *fatal* and *non*-fatal diseases. Should we be concerned only about the former (e.g., cancer, heart disease)? Just because the latter (e.g., shingles, Lyme disease, fibromyalgia) are not fatal, does this mean we can ignore them? Just because a disease does not kill us, does that mean it doesn't matter? NO!

Likewise, just because many or even most doctrines are not essential to salvation, this does not mean they do not matter. All doctrine is essential for *something*. *Whatever* the Bible speaks about, even if it is not an essential matter of faith and fellowship, the Bible HAS SPOKEN about it! And if the Bible has spoken about it, it is the WORD OF GOD. And if it is the Word of God, it has a specific meaning — the one God himself imbued it with. And we should be seeking *unity of belief* as to that meaning!

I say to you reductionist Peter Pans: GROW UP! Truthify in love!

A final enemy of sound doctrine, and source of the Peter Pan Syndrome, is simple doctrinal *laziness*. This is true of those who do not like hard work. Doing theology, they say, is just too hard! This is like a parent who says it is just too much trouble to fix meals for the kids — so they can just eat junk food! (Would sermons copied from the internet be the equivalent of junk food?) In response to this I will simply quote Hebrews 5:11 – 6:2:

> About this we have much to say, and it is hard to explain, since you have become dull of hearing. For though by this time you ought to be teachers, you need someone to teach you again the basic principles of the oracles of God. You need milk, not solid food, for everyone who lives on milk is unskilled in the word of righteousness, since he is a child. But solid food is for the mature, for those who have their powers of discernment trained by constant practice to distinguish good from evil. Therefore let us move beyond the elementary teachings about Christ and be taken forward to maturity, not laying again the foundation of repentance from acts that lead to death, and of faith in God, instruction about cleansing rites, the laying on of hands, the resurrection of the dead, and eternal judgment.

In other words, GROW UP! Kiss Peter Pan goodbye! Truthify in love!

CONCLUSION

Is church growth your thing? I hope so! And I hope you want your church to grow in the way Paul explains it should, here in Ephesians: We GROW UP by studying, knowing, agreeing on, and speaking out about sound Biblical doctrine and theological truth!

IS THE RESTORATION MOVEMENT STILL RELEVANT?

IS THE RESTORATION MOVEMENT STILL RELEVANT?

INTRODUCTION

The Restoration Movement developed in the early decades of the nineteenth century with the mission of restoring New Testament Christianity around the dual themes of UNITY and TRUTH. It has had an interesting and rather stormy history since that time. Around the early twentieth century it took three different paths. One was the liberal Disciples of Christ movement, which emphasized unity and abandoned truth. For the most part it has slid into irrelevance. Another path was the ultra-conservative churches of Christ, who admirably held fast to truth but for the most part abandoned unity. This is the group that eschewed musical instruments in their worship services, and who chose to be satisfied in their isolation from the rest of Christendom.

The third group has been called the centrist path of the Restoration Movement. This has been my home since my birth. I grew up in the Minorsville (KY) Christian Church, and received two bachelor's degrees (A.B. and Th.B.) from one of its premiere schools at that time, The Cincinnati Bible Seminary. I went on to teach theology in this same school for over forty-eight years. During my whole life I have sensed that our branch of the Movement is still trying to fulfill the dual purpose of its origin: to help bring about *unity* in Christendom by being faithful to the *truth* of the Bible.

We do emphasize the unity of Christendom, seeking to fulfill the prayer of Jesus in John 17:21, "that they may all be one." We are seeking to accomplish this by restoring a common commitment to the truth or sound doctrine of the Bible, especially the New Testament's teaching about the Church. Our plea is "getting back to what the New Testament teaches about salvation, church structure, and Christian living," or "going back to the New Testament for our doctrine and structure," says Ben Merold ("The Restoration Ideal Still Works," *Christian Standard*, July 2017, p. 53).

In the last few decades, though, questions have often been raised as to whether or not the Restoration Movement (I am speaking of its centrist path) is still relevant. Are we still faithful to our original goal? Are we having any success at it, or any impact on the Christian world in general? Is the Restoration Movement still relevant?

I.   KEY DISTINCTIONS DEFINED

Before I begin to specifically answer such questions, I will present some key theological distinctions that will be involved in my answer. (After teaching theology for over forty-eight years, I have learned to define theology as "the art of making proper distinctions.")

A.   *Obeying the gospel* as distinct from *obeying the law*.

First, we will distinguish between what it means to *obey the gospel* and what it means to *obey the law*.

Two New Testament texts refer to obedience to the gospel. Romans 10:16, where Paul speaks of the unsaved Jews of his day, says, "But they have not all obeyed the gospel." I.e., this is why they are lost. Then in 2 Thessalonians 1:8 Paul says that at His second coming Christ will be "dealing out retribution to those who do not know God and to those who do not obey the gospel of our Lord Jesus."

The fact that one must obey the gospel in order to be saved shows that the gospel includes *commands* in addition to facts and promises. These gospel commands are simply the Savior's instructions on what the sinner must do in order to receive salvation. They are very simple; the sinner is instructed to believe in Jesus as his Savior, repent of his sins, confess Jesus as his Lord, and be baptized for the forgiveness of his sins and for receiving the gift of the Holy Spirit. These gospel commands are the first four fingers of the old Restoration Movement "five-finger exercise." We do these things in order to be saved and to stay saved.

Obedience to the law is a different kind of thing. Every individual as a created human being is under a law code consisting of law commandments that must be obeyed, simply because God is our Creator and we are His creatures. Many of these law commands (i.e., the moral law) are the same for all people, but circumstances may change the full list of commands for different individuals or groups in different times. For example, the Jews between Mount Sinai (Exodus 19, 20) and the death of Jesus were under the moral law plus the Law of Moses. That was their law code. In the Christian era the law code has changed, though. No one since Christ's death has been under the Mosaic law; since that time all people (Jews and Gentiles alike) have been under "the perfect law, the law of liberty" (James 1:25). This New Covenant law code is simply the moral law plus all other New Testament commands on how to live a holy life pleasing to God. There are literally hundreds of such commands and instructions. These law commands are the last finger of the "five-finger exercise," i.e., "live the Christian life."

It is extremely important to see that the fifth finger of this five-finger exercise is not like the first four. Obedience to law commands is NOT how one becomes saved or stays saved. Jews in Old Testament times were not saved by obeying the commands of the Mosaic law; sinners in the Christian age are not saved by obeying the New Covenant law code. Obedience to law is not a condition for forgiveness of sins. Paul says clearly in Romans 3:28, "For we maintain that a man is justified by faith apart from works of law." In this statement, being justified is the same as being forgiven. Also, this is not referring just to the Mosaic law code, but to all law codes. There is no definite article ("the") before "law" in the Greek. The meaning of this statement is that sinners are not justified or forgiven based on how well they keep the law commands that apply to them, regardless of the age in which they live.

What does Paul mean when he says in Romans 6:14, "You are not under law but under grace"? Here he means that we are not under the *law system*, where salvation is based on perfect obedience to our law commands. Rather, we are under the *grace* system of salvation, where salvation comes through obeying the gospel commands. Paul is NOT saying here that we have no obligation to obey our law commands. The fact is that we human creatures are *always* obligated to obey whatever law code we are living under. The whole sixth chapter of Romans is making this point. We can see how important it is to make the distinction between obeying the gospel and obeying our law.

B.   *Faith* as distinct from *THE faith*.

In the second place, we need to distinguish between *faith* and *THE faith*. The New Testament words for the noun "faith" (*pistis*) and the verb "to believe" (*pisteuō*) are used in two senses. One is the *subjective* faith in the heart of the believer, i.e., the act of the mind or heart as it is performing the action of believing. This subjective faith can be a judgment of the mind directed toward statements or truth-claims in the sense of *believing that* they are true (e.g., John 20:31; Romans 10:9), or it can be an act of the will directed toward another person in the sense of *believing in* (or *on*) that person by surrendering or committing oneself to that person (e.g., John 3:16; Acts 16:31). This subjective faith, both in the form of "believing that" and in the form of "believing in," is the faith we exercise in order to be saved; it is one of the gospel commands required for salvation (cf. Mark 1:15; Acts 16:31; Romans 3:28; 10:9; Ephesians 2:8).

As distinct from this subjective faith, the noun "faith" is sometimes used in the New Testament in the *objective* sense. Here it refers not to *how* we believe, but to *what* we believe when we talk about "believing that" something is true. It refers to the body of doctrine we accept as true. It often has the definite article "the" in front of it: "THE faith" (*hē pistis*). Examples are Ephesians 4:13, which speaks of "the unity of the faith"; Colossians 2:7, which speaks of "being established in the faith"; 1 Timothy 3:9, which says that deacons must "hold to the mystery of the faith"; and Jude 3, which commands us "to contend for the faith that was once for all delivered to the saints."

C. *Unity of faith* as distinct from *unity of THE faith*.

When we speak of Christian unity, one aspect of this is unity as it applies to faith. This involves the previous distinction, i.e., between subjective faith and objective faith. Since subjective faith is an aspect of obeying the gospel, and since obeying the gospel is the gateway to salvation, all Christians have a "unity of faith" in the sense that all who have obeyed the gospel and are thus saved must have the *same faith*. I.e., all have believed and are believing THAT Jesus is the Christ, the Son of God (John 20:31) and THAT He arose from the dead (Romans 10:9). Also, all who are Christians have believed and are believing IN Jesus as their personal Lord and Savior (John 3:16). We are all united by this common faith.

On the other hand, there is also such a thing as "unity of THE faith," in the sense that all who are united in subjective faith are commanded to be united in *the* faith, i.e., united in the body of doctrine that we believe is true. I.e., we are supposed to *believe the same things* and *agree* on the one right meaning of God's Word. Ephesians 4:5 says there is "one faith," which most likely refers to this objective faith. This conclusion is supported by verse 13 in this same chapter, which says we are to keep striving "until we all attain to the unity of the faith and of the knowledge of the Son of God." Paul issues the same command in 1 Corinthians 1:10, thus: "Now I plead with you, brethren, by the name of our Lord Jesus Christ, that you all speak the same thing, and *that* there be no divisions among you, but *that* you be perfectly joined together in the same mind and in the same judgment" (NKJV).

Here is a key element of the distinction between these two kinds of unity. All Christians have the "unity of (subjective) faith," since we would not be Christians if we did not have it. We do not have to strive for this unity. However, the unity of *objective* faith is *not* something that just naturally exists among all saved people. We all become Christians with gaps in the content of our faith, and we come to believe different things about many doctrines, even important ones. This is the area where we need to work toward "the unity of the faith."

D. *The invisible church* as distinct from *the visible church*.

Finally, we must distinguish between what are called the *invisible* church and the *visible* church. The words "invisible" and "visible" are referring to what we human beings can and cannot see. I.e., there is something about the church that is invisible to human beings, and something about it that is visible to us. Specifically, regarding the invisible church, all who have obeyed the gospel — all who have the same saving (subjective) faith — are part of the one body of Christ, which is the church *as it is visible to and known only by God*. Its *boundaries* are *invisible* to us finite human beings. Only God knows for sure who is part of it and who is not.

On the other hand, the *visible* church is the church as mankind sees it. It is visible in the world and to the world. It is what people think of when they hear the word "church." The big problem is that in terms of what is available to our knowledge, this "visible" church is divided up into all sorts of different groups, with different names, different forms of government, different terms for membership, and of course many differences in their objective faith (*what* they believe).

II. THE RELEVANCE OF THE RESTORATION MOVEMENT

Now we are ready to address our main point: what does all this have to do with the Restoration Movement? How do these items help us to understand the relevance of the Restoration Movement in the Christian world today? How are we doing in reference to our goal of restoring unity by restoring truth?

A.   Relevance for the invisible church.

We will address this by using our distinction between the invisible church and the visible church. First, what is the relevance of the Restoration Movement to the existence of the invisible church? What have we done, and what can we do, to restore the unity of the invisible church? Actually, there is *nothing* we can do about the *unity* of it, because the invisible church as the body of Christ is *always* just "one body" of saved people (Ephesians 4:4). It already exists and always will exist. (See Matthew 16:18.)

This is true because all who obey the gospel are immediately "baptized into one body" (1 Corinthians 12:13); they immediately become and continue to be a part of God's family. This is true no matter what their relationship to the *visible* church may be. Those who have truly believed, repented, confessed Christ, and been baptized into Him are part of the invisible church, even if they never heard of "the Church of Christ" and are members (for example) of some Baptist or Roman Catholic congregation somewhere.

So if it has no relevance for the *unity* of the invisible church, does the Restoration Movement have ANY kind of relevance for the invisible church? The answer here is a strong "YES!" The one place where the Restoration Movement has had a very strong importance for the invisible church is in connection with its *membership*, i.e., who actually belongs to or is a part of this invisible church.

How is this so? We will remember that those who are members of the invisible church are those who are saved, and sinners are saved by *obeying the gospel.* I.e., they become members of the invisible church through faith, repentance, confession, and baptism. And I think there is no other group in the Protestant Christian world who has done more than the Restoration Movement to restore BAPTISM to the category of "obedience to the gospel," thus increasing the number of people who are added to the invisible church.

We must remember that up until and including the German Reformer, Martin Luther (d. 1545), all Christendom believed that Christian baptism was the moment of time when God bestows the double cure of salvation and thus the moment when one enters the body of Christ. Though perverted views had entered as to the *form* and *subjects* of baptism, as to its *meaning* it was considered to be a saving event. This was true until the Swiss Reformer, Huldreich Zwingli (d. 1531), totally separated baptism from the moment of salvation and began to teach that it is simply a sign of salvation that had already been received. Most Protestants followed this new path and accepted the Zwinglian heresy about baptism. Since his time, most Protestants have not received baptism in order to become members of the invisible church. The Restoration Movement, at least until recently, has tried to restore the original New Testament meaning of baptism as a salvation event.

I say here, "at least until recently." The sad truth is that many who are still associated with churches and institutions that are historically rooted in the Restoration Movement have imitated Zwingli and have separated baptism from the moment of salvation. They are preaching and teaching baptism as a work of man, not a saving work of God. Whole congregations have openly switched allegiance from their Restoration Movement heritage to an Evangelical alliance, mainly over the issue of baptism. A much publicized example is Max Lucado, as seen in this report: "Lucado's church is Church of Christ — but not a typical Church of Christ. For starters, musical instruments are used (although there is still one a cappella service). Also, the church has a baptistic view of baptism — that is, that baptism isn't required for salvation. Recently, his church, which has some 5,000 members, even changed its name from "Oak Hills Church of Christ" to simply 'Oak Hills Church.'" (Taken from *Baptist Press*, "Max Lucado transcends Church of Christ beliefs," by Michael Foust, posted May 09, 2005, http://www.bpnews.net/20752/max-lucado-transcends-church-of-christ-beliefs.)

This is not an isolated example. I have heard many accounts of similar such secessions. I have also checked many Restoration Movement church websites, and have found that their descriptions of what they believe about baptism is thoroughly Zwinglian. Just now I picked a city at random and looked up a Christian church at random, to see what their website says about baptism. Here is the essence of it: "The Bible teaches that we are saved by grace through faith (Ephesians 2:8). Baptism is a public confession of that faith in Jesus to God, the church, and the world." This description is pure Zwinglianism, asserting that the essence of baptism is something the baptized person is doing, not something God is doing.

I must conclude that we will continue to be relevant to the invisible *church only as long as we keep faithfully teaching the Biblical doctrine of baptism*. We will LOSE — *are* losing — our relevance when we stop preaching baptism as a saving work of God, and start echoing the Zwinglian heresy of baptism as a non-saving work of man.

B. Relevance for the visible church.

We turn now to the relevance of the Restoration Movement for the *visible* church. Do we have any such relevance? As I understand it, this has been the focal point of our Movement from its beginning. Its earliest leaders saw the need of restoring the unity of the church in the eyes of mankind, sensing that its many divisions were a serious hindrance to evangelism. They also had a sense of the reality of the invisible church, recognizing that there are many true believers in the many denominations. But the very fact of being divided into many denominations and sects weakened the church's witness to the world. So the point was to bring all these true believers (the *invisible* church) into *one visible church* that could be united around the same faith (the same objective doctrinal beliefs).

At least to some degree there was a recognition that we must have unity not only in our subjective saving faith, but also in *the* faith – that is, a unity in our belief about WHAT the Bible teaches. This would include especially an agreement on what the visible church should look like. Here is why we put so much emphasis on "the New Testament church" (issues of church polity and practice, or as theologians say, ecclesiology). An example is the popularity of a 24-page tract by the early twentieth-century Restoration preacher, P. H. Welshimer, "Facts Concerning the New Testament Church" (Standard Publishing, 1925).

The quest for the unity of the objective faith of the visible church cannot stop with ecclesiology, though. To some degree it has been and is still acknowledged that this unity must include a "unity of the faith" in general. The New Testament itself exhorts us to work to achieve such unity. First Corinthians 1:10 was cited above: "Now I plead with you, brethren, by the name of our Lord Jesus Christ, that you all speak the same thing, and *that* there be no divisions among you, but *that* you be perfectly joined together in the same mind and in the same judgment" (NKJV).

Also in 2 Corinthians 13:11 Paul exhorts us to this same unity, "Finally, brothers, rejoice. Aim for restoration, comfort one another, agree with one another [literally, "think the same thing"], live in peace." In Ephesians 4:13 he says that God's purpose is that "we all attain to the unity of the faith and of the knowledge of the Son of God, to mature manhood." In Philippians 2:2 he says, "Complete my joy by being of the same mind [literally, "think the same thing"], having the same love, being in full accord and of one mind." The Apostle Peter adds this in 1 Peter 3:8, "Finally, all of you, have unity of mind [*homophrōn*], sympathy, brotherly love, a tender heart, and a humble mind."

The Restoration Movement started strong on this point by adopting these slogans about the authority of the Bible: "In matters of faith [or, essentials], unity; in matters of opinion, liberty; in all things, love"; and "Where the Bible speaks, we speak; where the Bible is silent, we are silent." Rightly understood and applied, this kind of thinking begets unity of sound doctrine.

Sadly, however, I believe that this is another place where we are losing our quest for unity, namely, as it applies to the visible church in the form of unity of THE faith. As I see it, in many areas of the contemporary Restoration Movement, we are losing our commitment to sound doctrine, and to the very concept of truth itself. Over and over we are being minimized and neutralized by doctrinal relativism and doctrinal agnosticism. We are hesitant to take strong stands on specific doctrines and interpretations of Scripture. We are told that insisting on uniting on the one true meaning of Scripture is arrogant and divisive. Many seem to think that moving sound doctrine into the background actually helps us to achieve more unity with the denominational world. I.e., the less we teach about specific and distinct doctrines (especially baptism), the more fellowship we can have with Evangelicals – those who have the same *subjective* faith.

One result is that many churches are adding transfers from denominational groups who still hold to the teachings of those groups. Thus, even within these *congregations* there is a lack of this unity that God commands. For the sake of church growth and harmony, preachers are reluctant to preach against false denominational doctrines for fear of offending their members. Thus, false doctrines continue to be held by those in the pews. Often, some of these become teachers of Bible classes and even elders in the congregation. Sometimes whole congregations take on new (non-Restoration) identities.

Here is just one example. Many years ago, I had a student in one of my theology courses who recited her personal experience in a term paper. When she became a member of one of our largest Restoration churches, she was required to take a "new members" class, taught by one of the church leaders. They followed a printed outline, which she showed to me.

In the section on baptism, the outline was quite doctrinally solid. But she said that the leader of the class did not believe what was written therein, and openly told the students in the class that it was not true and they did not have to believe it.

It is clear that such doctrinal relativism moves us *away* from Biblical unity, rather than *toward* it.

What is the cause of this loss of urgency concerning the unity of the faith in the visible church? Many things could be named, but I will limit the discussion to what I believe is the most prevalent justification being offered for this loss of commitment to truth, namely, a faulty understanding and definition of the terms "essentials" and "opinions" in our very popular slogan, "In essentials, unity; in opinions, liberty; in all things, love."

In the first place, many of our leaders have *limited* the "essentials" on which we must be united, to things that are "essential to believe *for salvation*." Only salvation issues are "essentials," and the rest are relatively unimportant. What are these "essential for salvation" issues? All of us will agree that they are relatively few in number. I would personally limit them to some things related to God, to Christ, and to salvation. But what about the rest of the Bible, which is by far the larger part? My personal conclusion is that *everything* in the Bible is essential for *something*, or it would not be there in the first place!

But this is not what we are seeing in many areas of the Restoration Movement. For example, here is what a Christian church website in the Cincinnati area says: "As far as we're concerned, the essentials are all about the identity and meaning of Jesus' life, death, and resurrection. In everything else, there is room for dialogue, with each other, with our culture and with Scripture." For another example, the preaching minister of one of our largest churches was once told by one of his members that his Sunday school teacher was teaching "once saved, always saved." The minister replied that the member should not be too concerned about it, since whether one believed this or not was not a "salvation issue."

This is happening more and more! If something is not essential to believe for salvation, it is negotiable, or not really important. In fact, it is often just moved over into the category of opinion. Thus in this way, the bulk of Christian doctrine (Biblical teaching) is being labeled as just "matters of opinion." In my judgment as a lifelong student and teacher of the Word of God, *this limitation of "essentials" is seriously wrong!* Everything in the Bible is essential to believe and to understand in its original meaning, simply because it is GOD'S WORD OF COMMUNICATION WITH US! (See my more complete discussion of this in my book, *Faith's Fundamentals: Seven Essentials of Christian Belief,* Standard Publishing, 1995; now, Wipf and Stock; pp. 16-22. Also, see the essay on pages 107 – 128 in this volume.)

This leads to the second (related) reason why we are losing our relevance for uniting the visible church, i.e., we have *expanded* the category of "opinions" to mean "whatever you as an individual believe about any subject." In the field of epistemology, this *is* one valid way to use the word "opinion," but it is not what the word means as it is used in our venerable slogan! In the slogan, "opinions" are limited to things about which the Bible has not spoken at all! They are things about which the Bible is silent! This is the only place where we have "liberty" to believe whatever we want to believe. Whenever the Bible *speaks* about *any* subject, it has *only one right meaning*; and we are all obligated to try to find that one meaning and agree on it. That is the unity of the visible church that we should be seeking.

When we do this, only then will we as the visible church be fulfilling 1 Timothy 3:15, and thus be "the pillar and foundation of truth," in one voice making the one faith visible to all the world.

THE NATURE OF
BIBLICAL AUTHORITY

THE NATURE OF BIBLICAL AUTHORITY: A CONSERVATIVE PERSPECTIVE

INTRODUCTION

A *conservative* by definition is one who is inclined to conserve or preserve the historical, traditional state of things. Thus the conservative view of the Bible is the orthodox or traditional view, as contrasted with newer views. (This does not imply an uncritical, unquestioning acceptance of tradition, nor a refusal to consider newer views.) To be more specific, the basic essence of conservatism *is* its particular view of biblical authority, namely, the view that is considered to have been the consensus of Christendom from its beginning until modern times. It is the view that defines biblical authority in terms of the truthfulness of the contents of scripture and that understands its contents to be revealed and/or inspired by God in such a way that it is basically without error.[1]

In the larger spectrum of contemporary theological views, such a conservatism would include practically all who call themselves "fundamentalists,"[2] and most who would be comfortable with the designation "conservative evangelical."

Within the spectrum of conservatism itself, there are extremes from which most would carefully distance themselves. This includes the radical fringe that attaches inspiration and inerrancy to such things as the 1611 King James Version or to the Hebrew vowel points. It also includes those who call themselves conservatives but who hold to a view of inspiration that does not entail at least the *concept* of inerrancy (regardless of their feeling about the word itself).

The other term to be defined is *authority*. In its most comprehensive sense, authority is the right to establish norms for belief and conduct, the right to command others to conform to these norms, and the rightful power to enforce conformity by punishing wrongdoers. Some would add that it is the right "to act…without consulting anyone or anything else."[3] Some would argue, as does Bernard Ramm, that "in a very real sense all authority is at root *personal*."[4] That is, authority is an attribute that applies only to persons. Christians would certainly affirm that all authority, in the above comprehensive sense, ultimately belongs to a personal being, namely, God.

Is it proper, then, to say that authority can be an attribute of a written document such as the Bible? Yes, but only in connection with the very first aspect of authority as defined above. A document as such cannot possess the right to *command* and to *enforce* and to *act*; these are things that only persons can do. But the authority of a document can properly be described as "the right to establish norms for belief and conduct" because this aspect of authority is inherent in *truth as such*, whether considered in connection with a person or in the abstract (as in a document).[5] R.P.C. Hanson distinguishes between *external* authority as "that attaching to a person," and *internal* authority as "the authority residing in convincing argument or weighty moral or spiritual example or experience."[6] As we shall see, in reference to biblical authority these two things cannot be separated.

Concisely stated, the authority of the Bible is its right to compel belief and action (i.e., to establish norms for belief and conduct).[7] The word *compel* is used in a moral sense only; it does not involve any kind of physical compulsion. Here it means "to persuade" or "to place under an obligation." The *right* to compel belief and action is not the same as the power to do so.[8] When the Bible compels belief and action, it does so by right. We affirm the Bible's authority in this proper sense when we say that it alone is our rule of faith and practice.

Our goal in the rest of this paper is to explain why conservatives believe the Bible has such authority, why it has the right to compel belief and action.

I. THE BIBLE'S AUTHORITY LIES IN ITS TRUTH.

In simplest terms, the Bible is authoritative because it is true. The most vital or crucial aspect of its authority is a function of its truthfulness. To the extent that it is true, it has the right to compel belief and action. To the extent that its truthfulness cannot be asserted, the Bible has no authority. Carl Henry says, "What guarantees the authority of scripture is their [sic] divine truth."[9]

Truth here is understood in the sense of correspondence with reality. A statement is true to the extent that it corresponds with the way things really are.[10] Some object to this concept of truth because perceptual or observational difficulties make it impossible to determine "the way things really are." This may be so in an absolute sense, but this is more of a technicality than a practical problem. In any case, the correspondence concept of truth is the only one that deserves to be called "truth"; this alone is truth in the literal sense of the word. To define truth in any other way is to define it metaphorically. Strictly speaking, truth is a property only of *propositions* (i.e., statements, affirmations, indicative sentences). These are called cognitive statements or truth-claims; they can be either true or false. Non-cognitive utterances include such things as commandments and questions, and are not properly described as either true or false, with the exception explained in the next paragraph.

When we speak of the truthfulness of the Bible, then, we are speaking only of those parts or those statements that are actually claiming to be true (i.e., to correspond to reality). A considerable portion of the Bible is non-cognitive, and some parts, though cognitive in form, are intentionally figurative or parabolic in essence. In general, the concept of truthfulness does not apply to these parts (which are nonetheless authoritative in the direct sense that will be discussed below). We do need to point out, though, that there is a real sense in which the category of biblical commandments falls within the scope of truth. This is the case because the Bible's commands correspond to an aspect of reality, namely, the moral reality of both God and man; and thus they are true in the sense of corresponding to reality. Thus they bear the authority of truth and have the right to compel action.[11]

The relation between truth and authority as set forth here applies to all truth, whether found in the Bible or anywhere else. It is a general principle that truth has the right to compel belief and action. *Any* true statement has this right, no matter who says it. Once a statement has been determined to be true, we are under a moral obligation to believe it (or to obey it, if it is a "true" commandment).

According to the conservative view, biblical authority is simply a particular instance of this general principle. The authority of scripture is a function of its truthfulness. Why should any specific biblical statement be believed (or obeyed)? Simply because it is true. Any part of the Bible that professes to be true but is not, actually has no authority; it cannot rightfully compel belief or action.[12]

Herein lies the basic weakness of non-conservative views, which generally see the Bible as having the right — or at least the ability — to compel belief and action, apart from the question of whether it is true or not. Such a view of authority may be called the functional or experiential view, because it says that the Bible's authority is its ability to function in a particular way (whether by intention or not).[13] Usually it functions to produce a certain kind of experience in the heart and life of its readers. To the conservative mind this is not true authority. A message may compel with *more* than its truth, which scripture does; but any message that compels *without regard* to its truth or untruth lacks authority, i.e., it has no *right* to compel belief and action. One cannot validly accept a statement as authoritative unless he or she knows or rightly believes it is true.

II. THE BIBLE IS TRUE BECAUSE IT IS THE WORD OF GOD.

Even if we accept the fact that truth is inherently authoritative, this still leaves us with a crucial question, namely, how can we be sure a given statement is true? Basically there are two ways to be sure. We can *know* it by verifying it ourselves (via experience or investigation) or we can *believe* the testimony of someone whom we have reason to trust.

For example, let's say that you have promised your daughter that if she gets all A's in her first full year of college, you will buy her a new car. At the end of the year she calls from college and says, "I did it! I got all A's for the year!" If you suspect that your daughter's self-interest might lead her to exaggerate, you can examine the grade report with your own eyes or even check with each of her teachers to verify the truth of the statement. But if you trust your daughter, her testimony alone is sufficient to convince you of this particular truth. Either way, being satisfied that it is the truth, you are then compelled to act and thus to keep your promise.

Our approach to the Bible is basically no different from this. Are its statements true? How do we know? One way is to verify them ourselves through our own research and investigation. Was there a king of Assyria named Sargon, as Isaiah 20:1 claims? Was there a king of Babylon named Belshazzar, as Daniel 5:1 claims? If he was king and Daniel was second only to him, how could Daniel be the "third ruler" in the kingdom, as Daniel 5:16, 29 claims? Was Herod really the tetrarch of Galilee in the fifteenth year of the reign of Tiberius Caesar, as Luke 3:1 claims? Was there really a man named Jesus who was crucified under Pontius Pilate, as the Gospels claim? Did He really arise from the dead, as claimed throughout the New Testament?

The truth (or possible falsehood) of biblical claims such as these can in principle be verified by archaeological research and historical analysis. Statements about historical events are statements about situations that leave an objective imprint in their wake. The unqualified success of biblical archaeology in uncovering much of this imprint is a well-known story.

Thus the historicity of many details of the biblical narratives has been established. Conservatives as a rule believe that an honest application of the ordinary rules of historical analysis to the biblical records is sufficient to establish the historicity even of the resurrection of Jesus.[14]

The problem with this approach to verifying the truth of the Bible is that it is so limited in its application. For one thing, though it properly applies to statements of a historical nature, only a small fraction of biblical claims about historical events have been (and probably ever will be) individually verified thereby. The fact that the evidence thus far uncovered seems to be unanimous in its support of the Bible's historical details certainly gives us a *prima facie* reason to trust its historical claims in general, but still the bulk of this material is without any direct or specific support whatsoever.

Another limitation of this approach (of investigative verification) is that it applies only to statements about objective, historical events. By its very nature it cannot verify the validity of commands; it cannot verify the truth of statements about the meaning or interpretation of historical events; it cannot verify the truth of statements about the future, such as prophecies and promises; it cannot verify the truth of statements about events in the spiritual realm. The reality to which such statements correspond leaves no historical residue to be discovered by even the most diligent archaeological or historical research. And it is immediately evident that these kinds of statements are the heart and soul of theistic and Christian faith.

This leads us to the other way of being sure that a statement is true, namely, accepting the testimony of someone whom we have reason to trust. Some non-conservatives have in fact approached biblical authority in this way by calling it the "authority of the eyewitness." I.e., because the Bible is the testimony of those who actually witnessed the crucial events of salvation-history, it has a unique authority based on chronological primacy.[15] Kelsey speaks of "the consensus view that scripture is authoritative because it provides our *normative link* with God's self-disclosure."[16]

Surely there is some validity to this approach. The word of an eyewitness is generally accepted as more trustworthy than second-hand or third-hand testimony. And certainly much of the narrative material in the Bible *is* described to us by eyewitnesses whom we have good reason to trust and thereby bears the authority of truth. But this approach to authority also suffers from severe limitations. With reference to many significant events the biblical records are not represented as being the testimony of eyewitnesses (e.g., the events of Genesis, the virgin birth). But even more serious is the fact that, as noted above, the Bible's most crucial truth-claims are not about historical events as such and thus are not observable by eyewitnesses.

Where does this leave us, then, with regard to the truth and thus the authority of statements that contain the very essence of Christianity? How can we be sure that "in the beginning God created the heavens and the earth"? How can we be sure that Jesus of Nazareth is truly "the Christ, the Son of the living God"? We may know from eyewitness accounts that Jesus died on a cross, but how can we be sure that "He Himself is the propitiation for our sins; and not for ours only, but also for those of the whole world"? How can we know that remission of sins is truly given in Christian baptism? How can we know that making a "graven image" of God is wrong?

These are not the kinds of things that can be established by historical investigation or by the testimony of eyewitnesses. Why, then, do we accept them as true? Because these and other such biblical statements are the testimony or word of someone we have reason to trust, namely, GOD HIMSELF. Here is the heart of the conservative view of biblical authority: The Bible is entirely true and thus authoritative because it is the Word — indeed, the very *words* — of God.

God is the ultimate authority in all aspects of the term. He has authority inherently just because of who He is: the transcendent, infinite, omnipotent, omniscient Creator. This inherent authoritativeness applies to His words. Any words spoken by God are *ipso facto* true, and therefore authoritative. They compel belief and action just because they are the words of God. Unlike the words of those whose authority is only delegated and thus derived, the authority of God's words is not relative; it is absolute.

This is why conservatives believe it is crucial to understand that the Bible is the Word (or words) of God: This is the ONLY WAY its truthfulness, and thus its authority, can be guaranteed in reference to those parts of its contents that are most crucial for our Christian faith. Here is the point of the traditional doctrines of revelation, inspiration, and inerrancy. Revelation and inspiration are the *reason why* the Bible can be called the Word of God, and inerrancy is the *result* of its being the Word of God.

To reveal is to disclose, to uncover, to unveil, to make known that which was previously unknown. God is the subject of revealing action in many different ways, including the disclosure of truth to and through His apostles and prophets. *Revelation* is both the act of revealing and the product of that act. The latter includes the body of divinely given truth communicated to us in the form of words. Large portions of the Bible are revelation in this sense, i.e., they are words formulated in the very mind of God and disclosed to us through His spokesmen.

Revelation thus includes the direct and indirect communication of truth from God to others. *Inspiration* is involved in *indirect* communication, i.e., when God uses a spokesman or prophet to mediate this revelation (or other truth) to third parties. Revelation can be given without inspiration; the latter becomes involved only when God uses spokesmen to pass His revelation along to others. Inspiration is His divine control of the spokesman's mind and mouth for the purpose of guaranteeing the accurate transmission of His revealed truth. Also, inspiration can be given without revelation; not every inspired statement is a revealed statement. God sometimes desires a person to accurately transmit certain facts and truths known to him by means other than revelation; thus God exerts His divine control just to guarantee the accuracy of that transmission. Thus we may define inspiration as the supernatural influence exerted by the Holy Spirit upon prophets and apostles, which enabled them to communicate without error or omission those truths, received through revelation or otherwise, that God has deemed necessary for our salvation and service. (This definition was passed along to his students by Professor George Mark Elliott, one of my teachers at The Cincinnati Bible Seminary.)

In light of this distinction and this relation between revelation and inspiration, we can rightly say that although not all of the Bible is revealed, it is all inspired. Both revelation and inspiration together or either by itself is sufficient to produce a message that is rightly called *the Word of God*. The revealed and inspired portions of the Bible are certainly the Word of God, but so are those parts that are not revealed but only inspired. Though the latter come from human experiences and reflections, they are so guarded by the Holy Spirit in their transmission that they have God's full approval and guarantee of accuracy.[17]

This is the sense in which the quality of *inerrancy* is ascribed to the Bible. Because it is God's revealed and inspired Word, it *must* be inerrant, because an all-knowing and upright God could not and would not allow any errors, either deliberate or unintentional, to remain in the work to which He has given His stamp of approval. Thus "God's Word" is by definition "God's inerrant Word."[18]

Descriptions of this view of biblical authority are often plagued by unfortunate extremes on the part of its proponents and unfair caricatures by its opponents. Most conservatives vehemently repudiate both. For example, virtually no conservatives hold to a dictation or mediumistic theory of inspiration, despite the persistent attempts of some non-conservatives to link such a view with inerrancy.[19] *Verbal* inspiration means that even the words of the Bible are inspired, and not just the thoughts; it does not entail the idea that they were inspired by some form of dictation.

Related to this is the accusation that the conservative view leaves no room for a human side to the Bible. Such a criticism is quite untrue, being based on the unwarranted notion that humanness *requires* the presence of errors. This is no more true than the idea that the humanity of Jesus would require Him to commit sin.

Another extreme is the idea that inspiration and/or inerrancy somehow applies to certain copies or translations of the Bible. Though some fanatical fundamentalists do claim that the King James Version is revealed, inspired, and inerrant, no responsible conservative would hold to such a view. These qualities apply only to the original text as produced by the original writers of scripture.[20]

To speak of the Bible as the Word (or words) of God does entail a commitment to the possibility and reality of *word revelation*.[21] Most non-conservatives object to word revelation on philosophical grounds.[22] They say, for example, that it is metaphysically impossible for the transcendent, infinite God to speak understandably to finite beings: "the finite cannot contain the infinite." Conservatives reply that what some see as the problem is actually the solution. Rather than being a barrier to verbal communication, God's transcendence is the very thing that makes it possible. Just because He is infinitely powerful and wise, He is able to bridge the Creator-creature gap with understandable speech. The fact that we are created in God's image prepares us to be on the receiving end of this speech.

A related objection is that any alleged word revelation would have to be deposited among human beings in particular historical and cultural contexts and thus would be limited by the relativities of such contexts. Since "the relative cannot contain the absolute," any such alleged revelations could not be absolute truth with absolute authority. Conservatives reply in two ways. First, this objection confuses truth with the *understanding* of truth. It is true that the contents of any statement are relative to the historical context in which it is spoken. But this affects not the truth and authority of the statement but only cross-cultural attempts to understand it. Thus historical relativity is a factor in biblical interpretation, not biblical authority.[23] This makes critical Bible study all the more essential, not to determine whether a particular biblical statement is true, but to determine what it means.[24] Second, this objection exaggerates the problem of cultural relativity, implying that it is all but impossible to have reliable communication across cultural boundaries. While such is sometimes difficult, it is seldom impossible. We do it all the time, and usually quite successfully. The phenomenon of translation from one language to another is an example of it, while the translation of the Bible itself into countless languages is an example of its success.[25]

The conservative concludes that there is no valid objection to word revelation as such, or to the Bible's being called "the Word(s) of God" on such grounds. But there is also a more direct connection: (a) the Bible is the Word of God, (b) therefore the Bible is authoritative *just because* it is the Word of God and by that fact alone, since *every* word that God speaks bears inherent authority.[26]

This latter point leads us to the bottom-line conclusion for conservatives: There is no qualitative difference between the authority of scripture and the authority of God. This does not mean that the two concepts are identical.[27] For instance, there is a significant quantitative difference between them, in that the authority of the Bible does not exhaust the totality of God's authority; the latter is much broader in scope than biblical authority alone. Qualitatively, however, there is no difference. This is true because there is no difference between the authority of a *person* and the authority of the *words* he speaks, whoever that person is.[28] It may be true that authority is personal, but there is nothing more personal than the words that come from the heart and mind of a person. Jesus shows this inseparability in His rebuke, "And why do you call Me, 'Lord, Lord,' and do not do what I say?" (Luke 6:46).[29]

The only way to deny that the authority of scripture is the authority of God is to deny that scripture is the Word of God in any real sense. This of course is what non-conservatives do. For example, in this Barthian or post-Barthian era many will affirm that Jesus alone is the *true* Word of God, while the Bible is the "word of God" only in some distant or figurative sense. This permits them to distinguish between the authority of the Bible and the authority of God (or Christ), the latter alone being called absolute.[30] The old platitude, "Our authority is a person, not a book," is heralded widely.[31] But this is a false choice, because the Book in question is the revealed/inspired Word of the Person in question. Carl Henry rightly says, "A divinely given word mediated by the Logos of God through prophets and apostles is just as authoritative as that spoken directly by the incarnate Logos himself."[32]

This leaves one final question to be discussed, namely how do we know the Bible is the Word of God? Critics accuse conservatives of circular reasoning at this point, declaring that their view of the Bible is established by deductive rather than by the preferred inductive process. The alleged circularity is said to take the form of beginning with (i.e., presupposing the truth of) the Bible's *general* statements about itself (e.g., John 10:35; 2 Timothy 3:16) and deducing therefrom the inspiration and inerrancy of each *particular* passage of scripture. For example, "All scripture is God-breathed; Genesis 1:1 is scripture; therefore Genesis 1:1 is God-breathed." Or, "Scripture cannot be broken; Matthew 1:1 is scripture; therefore Matthew 1:1 cannot be broken." The crucial part of the criticism is that the conservative assumes the truth of the general premise uncritically and thus bases his whole case on an unproven assumption.[33]

Is this a fair representation of conservatism? For the most part, it is not. We grant that many conservatives may think this way, being moved more by inherited piety than by reason. We recognize also that one major branch of scholarly conservative apologetics consciously adopts an approach similar to this. It is called *presuppositionalism* and is limited mainly to certain Calvinists who follow the likes of Cornelius Van Til and Gordon H. Clark. But we must insist that this is *not* the traditional or mainstream conservative approach to biblical authority.[34] There is no circular reasoning; there is no captivity to deductivism.

It is true that the first step in the process is to examine the Bible to see what claims the biblical writers make for the whole body of writings known as Scripture.[35] This is one of the main points of the many detailed studies of what the Bible says about revelation, inspiration, and inerrancy. Emphasis falls on such general statements as "Scripture cannot be broken" (John 10:35); "All Scripture is inspired by God [God-breathed]" (2 Timothy 3:16); and "No prophecy of Scripture is a matter of one's own interpretation, for no prophecy was ever made by an act of human will, but men moved by the Holy Spirit spoke from God" (2 Peter 1:20-21). Also emphasized is Paul's general characterization of the Old Testament as "the oracles [the very words] of God" (Romans 3:2).

But this is not the end of the matter; it is only the first step. Even if it can be established exegetically that such passages as the above do indeed claim that scripture as a whole is the inspired and inerrant Word of God, conservatives do *not* blindly assume that this is true just because "the Bible tells us so." Rather, the next step is to ask the question, "Are there any good reasons for believing that such claims are true?" Here is where *induction* enters, as these claims are examined inductively in the study of Christian evidences. This discipline looks for both internal and external evidence to support the Bible's claims to be of divine origin. It considers such things as the unity of the Bible, its fulfilled prophecies, its remarkable accuracy as determined by archaeology and historical investigation, and its internal consistency. Such facts and phenomena, cumulatively (i.e., inductively) considered, are taken by conservatives to be more than adequate grounds for accepting the Bible's general claims about itself. *Only* when such reasons have been given for accepting these general claims do we then go on to deduce from them the truth of the other individual parts of Scripture.

The full statement of the conservative case for biblical authority is as follows: I. The Bible is authoritative in the sense that it has the right to compel belief and action. II. The Bible has this right because it is true, in the sense that its claims correspond to reality. III. The Bible is true and can be confidently accepted as such because it is the Word — even the very *words* — of God. IV. That the Bible is the Word of God is accepted as true because it is established by inductive reasoning in the form of Christian evidences.

We should note carefully that this does not elevate reason to a role of authority higher than that of the Bible itself. To affirm this "would be to use the word 'authority' in a quite different sense," says Hanson. "*Reason is the means whereby we reach religious convictions, not the matter which affords the material for making our judgments.*"[36] That is, it is merely the means by which we determine what *is* authoritative and what is not. Ramm is more specific:

> Reason has been made a religious authority by some writers on the subject, but reason is a *mode* of apprehension. If reason apprehends the truth, it is the truth apprehended which is authoritative, not reason. A man's reason apprehends the authority of the state, or distinguishes a true from a false claim to authority. Reason lays bare the grounds for authority. But the object of reason is the truth, and authority rests in what is apprehended, not in the instrument of apprehension.[37]

In other words, we approach the Bible's claims to truth and authority just as we would approach similar claims from any other document or person. If someone claims to have authority over us, we ask for the evidence; e.g., "Show me your badge." The acceptance of authority on any level is a rational decision based on evidence. Thus, though he does not mean it in this same sense, Barr is correct to say that conservatism (or fundamentalism) "is actually a rationalist position."[38] This should not raise any eyebrows. As Henry says, "Evangelicals need not tremble and take to the hills whenever others charge us with rationalism, since not every meaning of that term is objectionable."[39]

Thus we do not accept the authority of the Bible blindly, but use our reason to identify and verify it as the Word of God and thus the very embodiment of divine authority in our midst. But once it has been so identified and verified, we are compelled to submit totally to it, even with our minds.

CONCLUSION

In the final analysis there are only two choices in our quest for a final authority: divine truth and human experience. Conservatives accept the Bible's authority because they see it as divine truth. That is, its authority is determined by its origin or source or *cause*. When non-conservatives reject the nature of the Bible as divine truth but still attempt to retain some concept of biblical authority, the only alternative is to locate that authority in the Bible's *effect*, i.e., in its ability to produce some kind of experience in, or have a certain kind of impact upon, those who read it or hear its message proclaimed.[40]

The problem with the latter approach is that it leaves us with no standard by which we can determine what is a valid experience and what is a misleading and destructive experience, and by which we can defend the Bible's ultimate authority over against the claims of its rivals. Depending on how it is understood, the Bible itself can produce a multiplicity of experiences; and many of these cannot be differentiated from the experiences produced by other religious books and leaders and even secular leaders at times. The Christian has no more reason to accept his experience as valid, along with the whole theological system built upon it, than does the Mormon, the Muslim, the Jehovah's Witness, the Buddhist, or the Occultist. We are left with religious relativism, where the natural conclusion is that "Jesus is not the only Savior," i.e., the only one whose Word can produce a valid experience.

To the conservative mind, unless the Bible is *true* it has no authority, no right to compel belief and action, and no ability to produce *valid* religious experience. Only a Bible that is objectively true prior to our experience of it can claim any authority over us and at the same time produce within us experiences that will prove to be eternally valid.

ENDNOTES

[1] Whether inerrancy has actually been Christendom's view from the beginning or whether it is a view articulated only in the later centuries of church history, is a question that will not materially affect our discussion here. Jack Rogers and Donald McKim support the latter view in *The Authority and Interpretation of the Bible* (San Francisco: Harper and Row, 1979), while John D. Woodbridge argues for the former view in *Biblical Authority: A Critique of the Rogers/McKim Proposal* (Grand Rapids: Zondervan, 1982).

[2] James Barr tends to use the terms *fundamentalist* and *conservative* interchangeably and says that fundamentalism involves the idea that "the doctrinal and practical authority of scripture is necessarily tied to its infallibility and in particular its historical inerrancy" ("The Problem of Fundamentalism Today," in his book *The Scope and Authority of the Bible* [Philadelphia: Westminster Press, 1980], p. 65). While acknowledging the many who hold this view prefer not to be called "fundamentalists" but rather "evangelicals" or "conservative evangelicals," Barr considers the latter terms inappropriate for those who hold this view of biblical authority and thus labels them all "fundamentalists" (*Fundamentalism* [Philadelphia: Westminster Press, 1977], pp. 2-5). We cannot accept this approach, however. Though their view of biblical authority may be the same, fundamentalists and conservative evangelicals differ significantly enough on other points to warrant different designations.

[3] William Barclay, *By What Authority?* (Valley Forge: Judson Press, 1974), p. 7. See also H. D. McDonald, "Bible, Authority of," *Evangelical Dictionary of Theology*, ed. Walter A. Elwell (Grand Rapids: Baker, 1984). He says, "In its personal reference authority is the right and capacity of an individual to perform what he wills" (p. 138). Such a right, of course, is inherent in God alone, though He may delegate such authority in restricted spheres to human beings (e.g., civil government, parents, church elders). Carl Henry says, "God alone is the absolute power of decision" (*God, Revelation and Authority, Vol. IV, God Who Speaks and Shows: Fifteen Theses, Part Three* [Waco: Word Books, 1979], p. 25). [Hereafter, Henry's work will be abbreviated as *GRA*.]

[4] Bernard Ramm, *The Pattern of Religious Authority* (Grand Rapids: Eerdmans, 1957), p. 14.

[5] Ramm distinguishes the category of *veracious authority*, or "the authority of veracity or truth" (*ibid.*, p. 12). He recognizes that this would appear to be an impersonal kind of authority, but says that even this derives ultimately from the person of God (p. 13). Sometimes the connection is only indirect, though: "Veracious authority is directly or indirectly the authority of a person" (pp. 25f.).

[6] R.P.C. Hanson, "Authority," *The Westminster Dictionary of Christian Theology*, ed. Alan Richardson & John Bowden (Philadelphia: Westminster Press, 1983,) p. 58.

[7] Millard Erickson says it is "the right of the Bible to prescribe the belief and actions of Christians" (*Concise Dictionary of Christian Theology* [Grand Rapids: Baker Book House, 1986], p. 21). Carl Henry says, "When dealing with authority we are concerned with necessity or compulsion, with what must be believed or must be done" (*GRA*, IV:75).

[8] Not everything that actually compels belief and action has the right to do so. Bullies may compel action by threat of physical harm; charlatans and demagogues may compel belief through charm or charisma alone. Even a document filled with mistakes and lies can compel belief and action if it is cleverly and persuasively written.

[9] *GRA*, IV:75. This statement would be true even without the word *divine*.

[10] Strictly speaking the correspondence is not between the words of a statement and the reality it represents, as if certain words inherently correspond to particular aspects of reality. All words are "conventional signs," as Carl Henry says (*GRA*, IV:106). The crucial correspondence is between the reality as such and our concept of it. A statement is true to the extent that it either represents or provokes a concept that corresponds to reality, in accordance with the meaning assigned to words by convention.

[11] Carl Henry notes, "Imperatives are not as such true or false propositions; but they can be translated into propositions…from which cognitive inferences can be drawn." For example, "Thou shalt not kill" means "To kill is wrong" (*GRA*, III:417, 477).

[12] The Bible's truth (and therefore authority) is not its only appeal to humankind. Especially, the truth of the Gospel has a non-cognitive appeal as well; it draws us emotionally and aesthetically and existentially as well as intellectually. In popular terms, it appeals to the heart as well as to the head. But a "gospel" that is not true (see Galatians 1:6-9), though it may be presented in a way that appeals to the heart, has no true authority. It is a pseudo-gospel.

[13] Carl Henry observes, "The current tendency is to redefine biblical authority functionally…. The Bible is said to be authoritative merely in the manner in which it operates existentially in the life of the believing community" (*GRA*, IV:68). Henry

gives numerous examples, citing often James Barr (e.g., his *Fundamentalism*) and David H. Kelsey's *The Uses of Scripture in Recent Theology* (Philadelphia: Fortress Press, 1975), which is itself a survey of non-conservative views. Cf. Henry, *GRA*, vol. IV: chs. 3 & 4.

[14] See, for example, John W. Montgomery's *History and Christianity* (Downer's Grove: InterVarsity Press, 1965).

[15] R.P.C. Hanson says that when "judged by modern conceptions of authority...the Bible will be considered as the unique witness to the acts of God in history by which he makes himself known to all men and demands their response" ("Authority," p. 59). W. B. Blakemore has said, "The authority of the New Testament lies in its primacy and uniqueness, not in infallibility" ("The Place of Theology in the Life of the Church," *The Scroll* 47 [Summer 1955], p. 22).

[16] Kelsey, *The Uses of Scripture in Recent Theology*, p. 47. Italics added.

[17] Carl Henry comments thus on the relation between inspiration and authority: "The Christian apostles affirmed not only the divine authority of scripture but also its supernatural inspiration. Any repudiation of divine inspiration as a property of the biblical text they would have considered an attack on the authority of scripture. In their view scripture is authoritative, because divinely inspired, and as such, is divine truth" (*GRA*, IV:68).

[18] Not all conservatives are comfortable with the term *inerrancy*, usually as the result of a misunderstanding of what is intended by the word. Thus a refusal to use the word *inerrancy* does not necessarily exclude one from the ranks of conservatism. The International Council on Biblical Inerrancy has attempted to clarify what is usually meant by the term. See "The Chicago Statement on Biblical Inerrancy," an appendix to *Inerrancy*, ed. Norman Geisler (Grand Rapids: Zondervan, 1979), pp. 493ff. (see especially p. 496). See also Jack Cottrell, "Dedicated to Scriptural Inerrancy: The Biblical/Theological Implications," *The Seminary Review* 30 (September 1984), pp. 95-99.

[19] An example of this kind of false representation comes from Charles F. Lamb, who says conservatives insist that "each word in the Bible...is dictated by God" ("The Only Creed," *The Disciple* [October 1984], p. 11.

[20] The original *text* is different from the original *manuscripts*. The faulty idea that inerrancy is irrelevant because it applies only to no-longer-existent "originals" confuses the two. It is true that the original *manuscripts* no longer exist, but with few exceptions the original *text* DOES exist, thanks to the science of textual criticism. Inerrancy is an attribute of the *text*, whether that text appears on the original manuscripts, in a present-day critical edition of the Greek text, or in a faithful

translation of the same. For a discussion of this point see Greg Bahnsen, "The Inerrancy of the Autographa," *Inerrancy*, ed. Norman Geisler, pp. 151-193.

[21] See Henry, *GRA*, vol. III, chapters 24-27.

[22] For an exposition of the non-conservative view see John Baillie's classic work, *The Idea of Revelation in Recent Thought* (New York: Columbia University Press, 1956). For a conservative evaluation of it see Ronald Nash, *The Word of God and the Mind of Man* (Grand Rapids: Zondervan, 1982).

[23] This is not to say that these two things can be absolutely separated. Myron Taylor has rightly said that "the authority of the Bible is exercised effectively only through biblical interpretation," and that "we are compelled to interpret that Bible if we expect to encounter its authority," for "the Bible's authority is in its meaning" (*The Lamp* 13 [May 1988], p. 1). That is to say, the authority of the Bible lies not just in its truth as abstractly and formally considered, but also in the *meaning* of that truth as intended by its author. Conservatives believe that in most cases this intended meaning can be discerned with reasonable certainty. (Cf. the Reformation concept of the *clarity* [perspicuity!] of scripture.)

[24] As Henry says, "In actuality there need be no objection to historical criticism or to form criticism per se.... They do not by any inherent necessity either erode or destroy it.... What accounts for the adolescent fantasies of biblical criticism are not its legitimate pursuits but its paramour relationships with questionable philosophical consorts" (*GRA*, IV:81). Thus we reject allegations (such as Barr's) that the conservative view "involves the repudiation of the results of modern critical modes of reading the Bible" (James Barr, *The Scope and Authority of the Bible*, p. 66).

[25] See Henry's discussion of this idea of "the radical relativity of all beliefs and values" in *GRA*, IV:53-67; 113ff. He declares that "culture may surely shape the beliefs of any given period, but it cannot decide the truth or falsity of those beliefs." He reminds the proponents of cultural relativism that they expect their own statements to be understood cross-culturally; thus they are inconsistent. "Whoever contends that revelation cannot be the carrier of objective truth transcending our social location in history claims a privileged standpoint of personal exemption from that dictum. Nothing in either history or culture precludes transcultural truth. If the relativist can presume to communicate truth that spans cultural boundaries when he affirms historical or cultural relativity, surely the absolutist can do so; moreover, he alone has adequate reason to do so if in fact God has intelligibly disclosed his transcendent will. The truth of God can be stated in all cultures; it does not need to be *re*stated in any culture except by way of linguistic translation and repetition" (p. 53).

[26] Bernard Ramm has said, "The Bible is authoritative because it is the *Word of God* (that is, it is part of the organism of revelation) and for no other reason" (*The Pattern of Religious Authority*, p. 38).

[27] Carl Henry says, "There is, to be sure, a sense in which we ought and must speak exclusively of God as the absolute authority, and acknowledge scriptural authority to be merely derivative and contingent" (*GRA*, IV:42).

[28] See Jack Cottrell, *The Authority of the Bible* (Grand Rapids: Baker Book House, 1979 reprint), pp. 91ff.

[29] Robert Lowery has made this fine statement: "Accepting the lordship of Christ and the authoritativeness of scripture go hand-in-hand. In every single area of our lives, Jesus, the living Word, is to be Lord. Correspondingly, is it not true that the Bible, the written Word, is to be the authoritative guide for what we believe and how we behave as Christians? Unless God has given us a Word that is trustworthy, we will have no court of appeal for deciding what is truly Christian and what is not. To deny scripture's authoritativeness is to deny ultimately Christ's authority." ("Acknowledging the Authoritativeness of Scripture," Part One, *Christian Standard* [September 2, 1984], p. 7)

[30] Fred Norris says, "The New Testament which we accept as our norm does not ask us to accept it as our final authority. It speaks of Jesus the Christ. It proclaims Him as *the* authority." ("Jesus Is Lord," *Envoy* [January 1977], p. 1)

[31] See, e.g., William J. Moore, "The Biblical Doctrine of Ministry," *Encounter* 17 (Autumn 1956), p. 387. See also Leroy Garrett, "The Nature of Biblical Authority and the Restoration Movement," printed version of a speech at the North American Christian Convention (Anaheim, CA: July 24, 1974), p. 1: "Authority is not in a book but in a person."

[32] *GRA*, IV:37. See the full discussion, pp. 35-40, 50-52.

[33] James Barr has voiced this criticism: "To a very large extent, the doctrinal statements of modern conservatives base their position about the Bible on one single point: The Bible is authoritative, inspired and inerrant because the Bible itself says so. Because the Bible itself says so, we have to believe it, and if we do not, then nothing in the Bible would have any value." (*Fundamentalism*, p. 260)

[34] See R. C. Sproul, John Gerstner, and Arthur Lindsley, *Classical Apologetics: A Rational Defense of the Christian Faith and a Critique of Presuppositional Apologetics* (Grand Rapids: Zondervan, 1984).

[35] Critics say that the Bible never makes any claims about itself "in general" or "as a whole," since all the biblical documents were not in existence when most of the specific claims were made. (E.g., see Barr, *Fundamentalism*, p. 78.) This misses the

point, however. The biblical claims do not necessarily refer only to certain specific documents in existence at the time, but to a *category* or *class* of writings known as *scripture*. For example, see how naturally 2 Peter 3:15-16, referring to Paul, lumps "all his letters" in the same category as "the rest of the scriptures." For a discussion of this point see Henry, *GRA*, IV:134ff.

[36] R.P.C. Hanson, "Authority," p. 59.

[37] Bernard Ramm, *The Pattern of Religious Authority*, p. 44.

[38] James Barr, *The Scope and Authority of the Bible*, p. 70. He says that "it is perhaps the only really rationalist position widely operative within Christianity today.... Nowhere is the rationalism of fundamentalist argument more clear than in the doctrine of the inspiration and infallibility of the Bible itself." (*ibid.*)

[39] *GRA*, III:480. It definitely would be objectionable in the broad sense in which James Draper uses the term, i.e., as anything that constitutes "the human mind as ultimate authority." He includes within this category classical philosophical rationalism, classical empiricism, and mysticism. (James T. Draper, Jr., *Authority: The Critical Issue for Southern Baptists* [Old Tappan, NJ: Revell, 1984], pp. 16f.)

[40] A typical example is James Barr, who says the Bible's authority lies in its ability to *function* in a certain way, in its ability to effect a faith-relation between man and God. It is the "meeting-ground for our encounter with God" (*The Scope and Authority of the Bible*, pp. 53-55). "The authority of the Bible [lies] in the meeting with Christ which it mediated, and not in the acceptance as true of the information or attitudes which it contained" (*ibid.*, pp. 57ff.).

ABOUT THE AUTHOR*

(Photo collage – left to right/top to bottom)

1. Dr. Cottrell taught theology at Cincinnati Bible Seminary for almost 50 years. (*48.5 to be exact*)

2. Cincinnati Enquirer article, circa April 1962. Dr. Cottrell was a busy young man – husband, father, preacher, teacher, and scholar student.

3. Dr. Cottrell and his wife Barbara and their three children, Russell, Cathleen, and Susan, 1967.

4. Dr. Cottrell grew up in Stamping Ground, KY, and his blood runs Kentucky Blue!

5. Dr. Cottrell received his Ph.D. from Princeton Theological Seminary in 1970.

6. A young Dr. Cottrell at his desk in 1972. His writing career was getting ready to take off.

7. Jackie Cottrell, valedictorian of his class at Cincinnati Bible Seminary, 1959, speaking in chapel.

8. Jack and Barbara (Gordin) Cottrell were married in Grape Grove, OH, in 1958.

9. In addition to teaching, Dr. Cottrell spent many Sundays preaching and teaching in the local church.

10. Young Jackie working on his swing at the family farm in rural Kentucky. He is a big sports fan, and in addition to University of Kentucky sports, he enjoys watching the Cincinnati Reds, Cincinnati Bengals, and any NBA team that has a former UK basketball player on its roster.

---

*Photograph descriptions provided by Cathleen Cottrell.

THEME OF ROOTS
1. Justice
2. Righteousness
3. Gentleness
4. Save

The Ministry His Destiny

Young Man of Many Talents

BY BETTY DONOVAN

Jack Warren Cottrell, a candidate, somewhat shy twenty-man from Stamping Ground, Ky., has maintained an A-plus average at the University of Cincinnati, won a Phi Beta Kappa key, served as minister of the Mohawk Church of Christ near New Richmond and has been an instructor at Cincinnati Bible Seminary.

He also has been a loving father to Russell (Rusty), 14 months, and a devoted husband to Barbara Cottrell.

He explains his record in work...
...personal conviction...
...wants to serve...
...to...

- WILDCATS -

IAM-4UK

N,KY.

VIR VITA INCULPATUS

LITTERIS INSTRUCT

STUDIIS THEOL

SE IUSTO EXAMINE

DIGNUM HONORE PUBL

IDCIRCO NOTUM SIT QUO

Philosophiae Doctorem

CREARI VOLUIMUS

CUIUS REI HAEC MEMBRANA SIGILLO SCHOLAE NOSTRAE RATA

ET NOMINIBUS PRAESIDIUM NOSTRORUM MUNITA

TESTIMONIO SIT

TRUE
LIGHT

Made in the USA
Columbia, SC
28 October 2018